REFACTORING

A JOURNEY TOWARDS THE PINNACLE OF SUCCESS
AND FULFILLMENT AS A PROGRAMMER

CHIRAG KANSARA

Made with ♥ on the Notion Press Platform
www.notionpress.com

Contents

Contents

Contents

Foreword

Refactoring Your IT Career: A Journey Towards The Pinnacle of Success and Fulfillment as a Programmer" is more than just a book; it's a roadmap to a fulfilling career in the tech industry. It's not about quick hacks or shortcuts but rather a sincere and thoughtful examination of your own capabilities, interests, and potential as a programmer.

Throughout this book, we will embark on a journey that explores the various facets of a career in IT - from the initial days of discovery to the later stages of leadership and entrepreneurship. We will share the experiences, insights, and lessons that can help you navigate your professional journey more effectively and fulfilling.

Just like refactoring in programming, where we restructure existing code to improve its readability, performance, or 'code health' without changing its external behavior, this book aims to help you 'refactor' your career. To inspire you to make iterative improvements to enhance your professional growth while preserving your core passion for technology.

However, this isn't a one-size-fits-all guide. It's a compilation of personal experiences, insights, and lessons learned. Everyone's journey in the IT world is unique. This book encourages you to draw your conclusions, adapt the advice to your context, and pave your path towards the pinnacle of success and fulfilment in your programming career.

Remember, I am not an authority or expert but rather a fellow traveller in the IT world who is still learning and growing. By sharing my journey, I hope you'll be inspired and equipped to start refactoring your career. Here's to our shared adventure in the world of IT!

Chirag Kansara

Preface

This book began as a simple reflection. A reflection on a career that started with a modest salary of INR 1500 a month and progressed to a point where I led teams, created technology solutions, and made impactful decisions. Much like many others, my journey has been a mix of exhilarating successes and sobering failures, full of learning and unlearning. And it was this very journey that inspired me to write this book.

This book aims not just to serve as a manual for aspiring IT professionals but also to offer an honest and relatable insight into the joys, challenges, and nuances of a career in this dynamic field. The book combines technical advice with the soft skills required to succeed in the IT industry.

Starting with the thrill and anxiety of your first job, we move towards understanding the intricacies of entrepreneurship and timing your start-up. Then, we delve deeper into what I believe is a key skill often overlooked - the ability to enjoy life truly. We also discuss health, a paramount yet often ignored factor, especially in the IT sector. And finally, we conclude with a final word of encouragement and wisdom.

This book amalgamates years of experiences, conversations, and reflections. It's the book I wish I had when I started my journey. As you navigate through these pages, I hope that you find the insights and advice valuable, the anecdotes relatable, and the journey inspiring.

Whether you are just starting your journey or are midway, I hope this book helps you navigate your career and personal life with a little more insight and confidence. I hope it encourages you to cherish the small victories, learn from the setbacks, and most importantly, to remember that growth is a continuous process that requires both patience and persistence.

Thank you for choosing this book. I wish you a fruitful and enlightening journey.

Let's get started.

Acknowledgements

Writing this book has been a remarkable journey, one that I could not have undertaken without the support, encouragement, and contributions of many individuals.

First and foremost, I would like to express my deepest gratitude to my family, who have always been my pillar of strength and my source of inspiration. Their unwavering faith in my capabilities and constant encouragement have made this endeavor possible.

I would like to extend special thanks to my dear friend and mentor, Ram Chhawchharia. His wisdom, friendship, and guidance have been invaluable throughout my career. His ability to simplify the most complex issues and his deep understanding of the tech world have been an inspiration. Frankly, I believe he could write an even better book on this topic than me.

To all my past and present employers, I express my heartfelt gratitude for providing me with opportunities to learn and grow. The teachings and guidance you have provided me throughout the years have been instrumental in shaping my career and are reflected in the pages of this book.

To all my current and past employees, thank you for your trust, dedication, and hard work. You have been the wind beneath my wings, helping me navigate through tough waters and challenging times. This book is as much yours as it is mine.

My appreciation also extends to my publisher, for their trust in my vision for this book, and the editorial team, whose patience, guidance, and diligence have greatly enhanced the quality of this work.

Finally, I would like to express my gratitude to the readers and supporters of this book. Your engagement, feedback, and enthusiasm are a source of motivation. I sincerely hope that this book adds value to your personal and professional journey.

In conclusion, while I am the author of this book, it is a collective effort, a combination of many voices, experiences, and insights. Thank you all for making this journey possible.

Prologue

n a world where technology shapes our lives in ways big and small, a career in the IT field is both a challenging and rewarding path. It is an ever-evolving landscape, always demanding adaptability and continuous learning. If you are at the beginning of this journey, you might be filled with a mix of excitement and apprehension. If you are midway, you might be contemplating what next. Regardless of where you are on this journey, this book aims to be a guiding light, offering wisdom drawn from personal experiences and shared learnings.

When I started my career in the IT industry, my first salary was a modest INR 1500 per month. It was a humble beginning, and like many of you, I had dreams and fears in equal measure. Over the years, with every new assignment, I learned something new, and with each new challenge, I grew not just as a professional but also as an individual. I had my share of failures, but each setback was a stepping stone to a bigger success.

This book is a reflection of that journey. A journey that was not always smooth, but was always educational. Through these pages, I have tried to share the lessons that I have learned, the skills that I have honed, and the wisdom that I have gained. But more importantly, this book is about you - your aspirations, your challenges, and your journey in the exciting world of IT.

From surviving your first job, becoming an entrepreneur, to finding the right balance between your professional and personal life, this book covers it all. It's not just about the technical skills you need but also about understanding and navigating the dynamics of the IT industry.

So, whether you are a student, a novice programmer, an aspiring entrepreneur, or a seasoned professional looking for some perspective, this book is for you. It is a companion for your journey, a guide for your challenges, and a cheerleader for your victories.

Welcome to the beginning of an exciting journey. Let's turn the page and start our adventure.

Shall we begin?

Disclaimer

The views and opinions expressed in this book are the author's own, based on personal experiences and observations. They are not intended to malign any religion, ethnic group, organization, company, individual, or anyone or anything. The advice and tips in this book are for informational purposes only and are not substitutes for professional advice.

While every effort has been made to ensure the accuracy of the information contained in this book, the author assumes no responsibility for errors or omissions or damages resulting from the use of the information contained herein.

This book does not guarantee any specific results as the outcomes are based on various personal and individual factors. Readers are advised to use their discretion before making any decisions based on the information provided in this book.

All names, logos, brands, and other trademarks featured or referred to within this book are the property of their respective trademark holders. This book is not affiliated with or endorsed by any of these trademark holders.

The stories and anecdotes in this book are based on the author's personal experiences, and any resemblance to actual persons, living or dead, or actual events is purely coincidental.

By reading this book, you agree that the author and the publisher will not be held responsible for any repercussions or damages caused by implementing any of the advice or information provided in this book.

Please consult with a professional where appropriate and consider your unique circumstances before applying the advice provided in this book.

CHAPTER I

The Not-So-Fairy Tale Side of IT - Proceed with Caution

Ultimately, some of your greatest pains become your greatest strengths." - Drew Barrymore.

This book, titled "Refactoring: A Journey Towards The Pinnacle of Success and Fulfillment as a Programmer, " is your road map through the fascinating yet challenging terrain of the tech industry. The goal of this book is not to gloss over the hardships but to equip you with the necessary skills and insights to navigate them, thereby helping you build a successful and fulfilling career.

Refactoring, in the context of programming, involves restructuring an existing body of code while preserving its functionality. It's about improving the nonfunctional attributes of the software, making it easier to maintain and understand, thereby increasing its lifespan and adaptability.

Just as with code, refactoring your career is a continuous process. There's always a tweak or an optimization there that can make your work life a little better and more enjoyable. But remember, I am not an expert or authority providing definitive advice. I am simply a fellow traveller in the IT world, sharing my experiences and the lessons I've learned along the way.

In sharing my journey, I am making my conclusions and interpretations and fully aware that I could be wrong. That's the thing about personal experiences; they're just that - personal. Your journey might look quite different from mine, and that's perfectly okay.

What's important is that you reflect upon your own experiences, draw your conclusions, and make decisions that best suit your personal and professional goals. Use my words not as an infallible guide but as a source of ideas and inspiration.

In a typical narrative, you'd expect me to start by enticing you with the glittering allure of the IT world. Talk about the inspiring success stories, the triumphs, the breathtaking innovation, and all the marvellous things that make the IT industry a beacon for young, ambitious minds.

But this isn't my typical narrative.

As they say, "Before every great success, there's usually great caution." So, let's flip the script and look at what's often kept in the background - the challenges, the hurdles, and the not-so-glamorous parts of working in IT.

Why this unusual approach, you might wonder?

Because this isn't a sales pitch, this is an honest account, and honesty warrants a full view of the landscape, complete with its mountains and valleys.

So, before we embark on this thrilling journey through the expansive IT terrain, let's ensure we're fully equipped. Let's take a moment to acknowledge and understand the roadblocks in our path.

After all, a well-prepared traveller is far more likely to enjoy a successful journey. Brace yourself because we're about to expose the rough terrains that often stay hidden behind the sparkling façade of the IT kingdom.

CHAPTER II

Unravelling Your IT Affinity: A Quest for Your Programming Potential

"Knowing yourself is the beginning of all wisdom." - Aristotle.

Once upon a time in the magical kingdom of IT!" It sounds like a charming fairy tale, right?

The tech industry is full of exciting possibilities and stories of young prodigies who succeed among technology giants. It's a world where talented individuals work with fascinating codes and algorithms and are rewarded with good-paying jobs and innovative work environments. For those who are brave enough to explore this world, a bright future awaits.

No wonder many science and engineering graduates are queuing to punch tickets for this coveted IT express. But let's pump the brakes and park the hype train.

• • •

Is IT truly a one-size-fits-all profession?

• • •

Can every aspiring Jack and Jill morph into a proficient software developer, designer, or architect by simply choosing a career in IT?

• • •

The short answer: not quite.

• • •

The intricate world of IT, just like any other profession, demands a specific skill set, the right mindset, and, yes, an inherent knack.

The IT universe might lure you in, but the question is, are you suited to be a part of it? That's the million-dollar question we need to explore.

For every resounding success story of an IT maven making waves, countless others dabbled, struggled, and eventually retreated from the IT battlefield, their aspirations and dreams not finding their rightful place.

What's the deal-breaker? Often, the absence of certain essential traits is required to thrive in this challenging yet rewarding landscape.

There's no shame in recognizing that IT isn't your calling. By the end of this chapter, you'll have a clearer understanding of your compatibility with this field. So, are you ready to embark on this enlightening journey and navigate the often-turbulent waters of the IT ocean? Let's set sail!

Think about it this way: becoming a programmer is like stepping into a professional arena. Just like you can't be a top-notch lawyer or an exceptional teacher without the necessary aptitude, the same principle applies to the IT industry.

It may look alluring from the outside, but you'll never find true satisfaction or excel in your work if you lack the right attributes.

Programming, my friend, is akin to the art of baking. You don't necessarily need a fancy degree/diploma to be a coding genius, but you do need a foundation of basic cognitive skills.

As we close this chapter, it's clear that being part of the IT kingdom isn't merely about being enticed by its charm. It involves understanding if you truly resonate with the nature of the work, the thought process, and the specific skills it demands. It's about uncovering your affinity for IT and discerning whether this is a field where you can thrive and enjoy your work.

But how do we determine this fit? How can we choose if we have the potential for programming, a crucial aspect of the IT world?

Well, dear reader, your patience is about to be rewarded. In the next chapter, "Discovering Your Programming Potential," we'll delve into unravelling your programming capabilities and inclinations.

CHAPTER III

Discovering Your Programming Potential

""Everybody in this country should learn to program a computer, because it teaches you how to think." - Steve Jobs. "

In this chapter, aptly titled "Discovering Your Programming Potential," we will delve into the intricate aspects that can determine your aptitude and passion for programming. We will examine the nuances that separate those who enjoy and succeed in programming from those who struggle with or have little interest in it.

Well, now, isn't it intriguing? There's no cookie-cutter, one-size-fits-all mould for what a 'programmer' should look like. Trust me on this one; I'm living proof!

People hailing from every nook and cranny of life, brandishing a wide range of skills, have cracked the code (pun absolutely intended) and found success and joy in the programming universe.

But don't get me wrong, a few quirks and traits could give you a leg up in this realm. It's like having a secret cheat code in a video game. Specific cognitive abilities and personality characteristics can turbocharge your potential in this intriguing world of bits and bytes.

But don't worry; it's not about turning you into a human computer; it's about making the computer an extension of your creativity.

We'll soon delve into some essential traits that often come in handy in the realm of programming. Aligning these traits with your own can provide insight into your potential as a programmer.

This might seem a bit overwhelming initially but don't worry. Remember the old saying, "A journey of a thousand miles begins with a single step."

The truth is out, and it's not so grim after all! Programming is an art; like any art, it requires passion and potential.

So, you've unlocked the first part of the puzzle; what's next, you ask? Imagine opening Pandora's box filled with mysteries. Intrigued?

Fasten your seatbelt, and let's embark on solving the 'Great Programmer Potential Puzzle'!

CHAPTER IV

The Great Programmer Potential Puzzle

""Give a man a program, frustrate him for a day. Teach a man to program, frustrate him for a lifetime." - Muhammad Waseem"

Welcome, dear reader, to "The Great Programmer Potential Puzzle," a chapter sure to be as entertaining as it is enlightening. Remember, programming isn't just about debugging a code at 3 AM with a lukewarm coffee by your side (though that happens more often than you'd think!).

The fascinating realm of programming, where imagination and logic unite to sculpt the digital landscape, is no mystery to us anymore.

However, As we proceed, it's time to delve deeper. The next stage of our journey is not about the art of programming but the artist behind it.

Is programming everyone's cup of tea, or does it demand a specific palate to relish its flavor truly?

Research has suggested that not everyone carries the natural propensity to grasp the art of programming. A little intimidating. But don't fret, for every cloud has a silver lining.

Our goal in this chapter is to peel back the layers, unravelling the essence of programming aptitude.

So please sit back, relax, and let's embark on this expedition to discover your hidden programming potential. Who knows, by the end of this chapter, you might even find yourself eager to tackle that 3 AM debugging session!

By honestly evaluating your interests, aptitudes, and preferences, you can gain clarity and make informed decisions about your professional journey.

Alright, brace yourselves! We're about to embark on a thrilling journey through a maze of research that reveals why the mystical art of programming eludes some of us. If you do not appreciate the beauty of logic or have a sworn vendetta against proof, you might want to skip this section.

But hey, who doesn't love a good dose of reality served with a dash of scientific evidence, right? ?

Saeed Dehnadi, a reputable researcher (check out his work at https://www.eis.mdx.ac.uk/research/PhDArea/saeed/), has delved into this very topic. And guess what? His findings align with previous studies.

Programming, my friend, is not a universal gift bestowed upon all. It takes a specific breed of individual to grasp and absorb programming concepts swiftly. However, fear not, for anyone can learn to code with the right mindset and great effort.

In the realm of programming, there's a famous paper floating around that seeks to determine who is indeed cut out to be a programmer. It's called "A cognitive study of early learning of Programming" by Prof Richard Bornat and Dr Ray Adams (here: https://www.eis.mdx.ac.uk/research/PhDArea/saeed/).

According to their research, the results showcase a curious phenomenon: a "double hump." It's as if there are two distinct populations—one group with the knack for programming and another that doesn't. Almost all attempts to improve programming education have focused on teaching methodologies, language changes, application areas, IDEs, and motivation.

Alas, none of these endeavours has effectively obliterated the double hump. However, fear not, for they have devised a test to discern the population with coding capabilities before even embarking on a course. I know it sounds implausible, but their findings are intriguing.

The exact mechanisms behind this phenomenon may remain a mystery, but they have some compelling theories.

Speaking of renowned figures in the programming world, let me introduce Jeff Atwood, the founder of stackoverflow.com, whose blog aptly bears the title 'Coding Horror' (learn more about him at https://blog.codinghorror.com/about-me/).

In one of his insightful blog posts (find it here: http://www.codinghorror.com/blog/2006/07/separating-programming-sheep-from-non-programming-goats.html), he candidly discusses the eternal truth that, despite the immense changes in the technological landscape, most people can't grasp the intricacies of programming. In fact, 30% to 60% of university computer science departments students fail their first programming course.

It's a harsh reality, but it underscores the fact that programming is not a skill easily acquired by everyone.

There's abundant research exploring how people can effectively and swiftly learn programming. A significant aspect of this process revolves around mindset and grasping the right mental models. It's not just about memorizing syntax and algorithms; it's about developing a programmer's mindset—a unique way of approaching problems and finding elegant solutions.

If you're considering the path of a programmer, let's pause for a moment and ponder a few essential questions:

- Did you find joy in playing chess or solving puzzles during your childhood? It's a sign of a mind wired for logical thinking and problem-solving.

- Do you genuinely enjoy mathematics? It's not about your math grades; it's about the inherent fascination and pleasure you derive from mathematical concepts.

- Are you the kind of person who thrives on trial and error? Can you endure the process of repeatedly trying and failing until you uncover the right solution?

- Are you willing to put in the extra hours and go the extra mile? Programming often demands persistence and a willingness to invest time and effort beyond the standard work hours.

- Do you find solace in unravelling intricate logical problems? Does the challenge of untangling complex webs of logic ignite a sense of excitement within you?

If you responded with an enthusiastic "yes" to these questions, then congratulations are in order! You possess the potential to embark on a satisfying and successful career as a programmer.

On the other hand, if most of your answers leaned towards "no," it might be prudent to reconsider your aspirations of becoming a programmer. That's not to say you can't pursue the field or even excel in it, but you'll likely find it challenging to derive genuine enjoyment from your work if most of your responses were negative.

So, my friend, reflect upon your inclinations and talents. Embrace the programmer's code if you possess the right mix of puzzle-solving prowess, a love for logical thinking, and a willingness to immerse yourself in the intricacies of code. And remember, whether you choose the path of a programmer or explore other avenues, success and fulfilment await those who align their passions with their chosen craft.

In conclusion, let me leave you with a fitting quote from a renowned figure in the world of programming:

"Everyone should learn how to program a computer because it teaches you how to think." - Steve Jobs

These words from the visionary co-founder of Apple encapsulate the essence of programming. It's not just about acquiring a technical skill; it's about cultivating a mindset that empowers you to tackle complex problems with creativity and precision.

However, dear reader, heed this warning: if you choose to continue becoming a programmer, do so with full awareness of the criteria and challenges that lie ahead. The journey may require countless hours of dedication, a hunger for knowledge, and the ability to embrace the ever-changing landscape of technology.

Only proceed if you possess the unwavering determination and passion to meet these demands head-on.

But if, dear reader, you find yourself ready and excited to embark on this extraordinary journey, then I invite you to turn the page and dive deeper into the realms of programming. The challenges you'll encounter will test your mettle, but the rewards will be equally grand. Prepare to unlock the power to create, to shape the digital world with your fingertips, and to join the ranks of those who harness the magic of code.

You have started solving the puzzle, haven't you? Fantastic! Programming Career is starting to look less like rocket science. But every great superhero must find their perfect fit and unique superpower. Will you be the Spiderman or the Black Widow of programming? Find out in the next chapter.

CHAPTER V

The Perfect Fit – Unleashing Your Inner Programming Superpower

""Always code as if the guy who ends up maintaining your code will be a violent psychopath who knows where you live.' - John Woods."

Brace yourself, code warriors, as we delve deeper into the rabbit hole of this thrilling world of programming in this chapter: 'The Perfect Fit - Unleashing Your Inner Programming Superpower.' But before we do, here's a quick joke: why don't programmers like going outside? The fear of bugs. Yes, bugs, but not the creepy crawly kind - the ones that lurk in your code, waiting to wreak havoc on your beautiful, logically crafted world.

Don't worry; the humour does get better. Or does it?

You're considering taking the plunge into this world, huh? Well, before you strap on your keyboard, let me tell you, stepping into the shoes of a programmer isn't like playing a round of bingo. You can't just sit back, relax, and hope for your number to be called.

You could certainly give that approach a shot. Still, odds are, you'd find yourself as exasperated as a JavaScript developer who's spent hours pouring over code that refuses to work correctly, despite appearing perfectly fine. Hint: It's always a missing bracket. Always.

In this chapter, we will embark on a voyage of self-discovery, exploring what it truly takes to unleash your inner programming superpower. Prepare yourself for an exciting roller coaster ride through the programming world's ups, downs, loops, and dramatic falls.

By the end, you'll have a clearer picture of whether you're ready to don your coding cape and take your place among the programming elite. So strap in, keep your hands inside the vehicle, and let the journey begin.

In the wild world of programming, a realm where semicolons become your nemesis, the phrase "it works on my machine" is practically a mantra.

So you want to dive headfirst into this world, eh? But let me tell you something; becoming a programmer isn't like winning the lottery. You can't just buy a ticket and hope for the best.

Well, you could try, but you'd probably end up just as frustrated as a JavaScript developer who can't figure out why his code only works 99% of the time.

There's an old programmer's adage that says, "Everyone can code, but not everyone should." It might sound harsh, but the idea is not to gatekeep the field. Instead, it's to emphasize that programming is a craft that requires specific skills and temperament.

This journey isn't for the faint-hearted. It requires patience, perseverance, and a passion for problem-solving. It's like a strategy game where you're both the player and the game maker.

So, let's start by identifying whether you've got the right chops for the job. In the world of programming, that's known as checking the prerequisites.

- Do you have what it takes?
- Do you find joy in solving complex problems?
- Does the idea of creating something from scratch excite you?

If yes, then my friend, you're in the right place.

And for those uncertain or answer with a resounding no, fret not. You might still have a place in the world of IT, just not in the programming corner. After all, this grand IT symphony has many instruments to play.

When I transitioned from a traditional job to programming, the world wasn't as connected as it is today. We didn't have the mighty Google at our fingertips, and information was primarily found in print. But they say that when you passionately desire something, the universe conspires to make it happen. And that's exactly what transpired for me.

Nowadays, deciding to pursue a career in programming is simpler than ever. The vast array of options is within your reach; it's merely a matter of making a firm decision and taking that leap of faith.

Drawing from my personal experience, allow me to delve into the qualities and skills that can transform you into a remarkable developer or programmer.

With a tenacious problem-solving mindset, unwavering patience in the face of challenges, adept communication abilities, a sprinkle of creative thinking, and an insatiable thirst for continuous learning and collaboration, you will embark on a journey of greatness in the realm of programming.

There's a superhero in all of us, waiting to take flight. You've now discovered your unique programming power. But what good is a superpower if you can't solve problems? Can we interest you in some problem-solving action? In the chapters that have passed, we may have explored some challenging aspects, and I apologize if I came across as pessimistic. I intended to prepare you for the realities that await you in your professional journey.

But, as we progress, I assure you the tone will be more optimistic. In the subsequent chapters, I promise to share insights that are unique and invaluable - insights that you may not find elsewhere.

If you've come this far, you will brave the rest of the journey. You've made it through the storm; now, it's time to navigate towards the rainbow. Your next mission awaits, and it promises to be an enlightening one.

Let's continue this extraordinary journey, and together, we will uncover the secrets of success in the IT world. Are you ready to take flight?

CHAPTER VI

The Problem is the Solution!

" "Problems are nothing but wake-up calls for creativity" - Gerhard Gschwandtner. "

Welcome to "The Problem is the Solution!" an insightful chapter exploring the art and science of understanding problems to sculpt innovative solutions.

Throughout my career, I've found that one crucial aspect often goes overlooked in our rush to generate results: understanding the essence of the problem. When discussing projects with clients, I emphasize the importance of comprehending the core issue they're trying to resolve.

This understanding forms the bedrock of effective team communication and efficient project planning. By burrowing down to the root of the problem, we can steer our team towards creating superior, more effective solutions.

Quite often, developers behave like foot soldiers on a battlefield, carrying out orders without truly grasping the larger strategic plan. They may neglect to fully understand the problem they're addressing or the project's broader requirements, focusing only on their specific assigned task. However, with a more profound understanding of the problem, we can foster a more innovative, solution-oriented mindset.

So buckle up, and get ready for a deep dive into the importance of problem understanding in the fascinating world of programming and how it can be the key to unlocking your team's creative potential. Because when you truly understand a problem, you're not just closer to the solution - you're standing right on top of it.

To truly enjoy your work as a programmer and experience the rush of dopamine while coding, you must comprehend the fundamental problem a specific project aims to solve. From there, you can build a solid foundation and proceed with confidence.

To stay ahead of the game, ask yourself these questions before embarking on any new project or task. The answers will guide your solution development, ensuring you don't get stuck in the quagmire of uncertainty further down the line.

Just like baking a cake, a successful project requires the right ingredients. You can usually find these answers in kickoff meetings or project charters.

The key lies in understanding the significance of each ingredient and how it contributes to the final product.

Let's dive into these questions with some real-life examples:

1. **What is the core problem that needs solving?**

Real-life example: A client complains about their website's high bounce rate. The core problem to solve here is why visitors leave the site without engaging with the content or making purchases.

1. **What is the most efficient way to accomplish this?**

Real-life example: To address the high bounce rate issue, an efficient solution might be to conduct a user experience (UX) audit and update the website design based on user feedback and analytics.

3. **How does each feature or task relate to the larger problem the project addresses?**

Real-life example: One task might involve redesigning the website's landing page to be more user-friendly. This relates back to the larger problem by aiming to decrease the bounce rate, thereby improving user engagement and potential sales.

4. **What are the essential features of this project?**

Real-life example: Essential features for the website update project might include an intuitive navigation menu, a visually appealing design, mobile compatibility, and fast loading times.

5. **How will the project owner generate revenue from this endeavour?**

Real-life example: The project owner might expect to generate revenue from this project by attracting more visitors to their website, increasing user engagement, and consequently boosting sales.

6. **What information do the project owner or stakeholders need to make informed decisions and evaluate business performance?**

- Real-life example: The stakeholders might need information like website analytics, user feedback, and sales reports to evaluate the success of the redesign and make informed decisions about future improvements.

By seeking answers to these questions, you can focus on critical tasks and derive genuine enjoyment from your work. It's like having a clear map in your mind when traversing a road; with clarity, you won't constantly question whether you're heading in the right direction.

A well-cracked problem leads to an innovative solution. You're starting to get the hang of this, aren't you? But remember, with great power comes great... patience. Ready to flex your patience muscle?

CHAPTER VII

Get Your Patience to Work!

""Patience is not the ability to wait, but the ability to keep a good attitude while waiting." - Joyce Meyer"

As we step into our new chapter, intriguingly titled "Get Your Patience to Work!", I'd like to highlight an essential, yet often overlooked, attribute in a programmer's toolkit: patience. It's a virtue, as they say, and in the realm of programming, it's the unsung hero behind many successful software.

My dear readers, programming is a roller-coaster ride of triumph and tribulation. It's a world where your code can sometimes seem as capricious as a toddler, refusing to work even when everything looks perfect. And this doesn't change whether you're a novice staring wide-eyed at your first "Hello, World!" or a seasoned veteran with decades of coding stories to tell. Rarely does a program run flawlessly on the first try - but therein lies the beauty of this journey.

You'll need a certain temperament for this line of work. Yes, you heard it right - it's completely okay to let out a colourful word or two when your code throws an unexpected error for the umpteenth time. But the trick is not to let this hiccup deter you from the path of perseverance.

The answer to our most vexing problem is often sitting right under our noses, but we're too entrenched in our struggles to see it. That's when you need to step back, take a breather, listen to soothing tunes, or even call it a night.

Returning to the problem with a fresh mind can make the elusive solution crystal clear. Remember this mantra: hold your patience close, and don't let the stress monsters nibble at your resolve.

So, are you ready to embrace patience and let it work its magic on your programming journey? Let's delve into the story further.

Programming is akin to navigating through a maze. It's a journey filled with dead-ends and wrong turns, where the path to the exit—your perfect code—often eludes you. As a seasoned programmer with a quarter-century of experience under my belt, I can tell you this: seldom will your code run perfectly on the first, second, or even third attempt.

Let me share a personal story with you. I worked on a crucial project for a high-profile client during my early years in programming. The complex project involved numerous interwoven modules that had to work in perfect harmony. After many sleepless nights, I was nearing the finish line. Or so I thought.

On the day before the final deployment, I found a bug in the system. I dove to rectify it, confident I could handle it quickly. Hours turned into a whole night, and I grappled with the same bug. Every attempt to fix it seemed to spawn a new error. Frustrated and exhausted, I felt like screaming at my monitor. Instead, I decided to step back and take a breather.

I walked away from my computer, took a nap, and woke up with fresh eyes and a rejuvenated mind. I IMMEDIATELY NOTICED AN OVERLOOKED DETAIL when I looked at the problem again. It was a tiny logic error that was causing all the trouble. Had I allowed my frustration to consume me, I might have missed it altogether.

This incident reminded me of a legendary story about Marie Curie, the renowned physicist and chemist and a two-time Nobel laureate. Legend has it that she struggled with a challenging research problem. Despite her best efforts, she could not find a solution.

She decided to take a break and get some sleep. In the middle of the night, she woke up with the solution suddenly clear. She hurriedly jotted it down and went back to sleep. When she woke up, she found the solution scribbled on a piece of paper beside her bed.

Both incidents illustrate the power of stepping back, taking a break, and allowing your subconscious mind to work on the problem. It's a lesson about patience, perseverance, and a clear mind. No problem is insurmountable if we approach it with the right mindset.

Frustration is natural when things go awry, and expressing it is okay (preferably not by hurling your laptop out the window!). However, it's essential to remain patient and not let momentary hiccups cloud your judgment or mar your perseverance.

The solution to a problem frequently stares us in the face, but our tunnel vision prevents us from seeing it. During these times, stepping away from the problem, taking a break, or even sleeping on it, can prove immensely beneficial. When you return, you often find that the solution was there all along, just waiting for you to see it.

In this field, patience truly is a virtue. It gives you the power to endure, persist, and ultimately succeed. Embrace it, and you'll find that programming isn't just about writing code - it's a journey of constant learning, improvement, and personal growth.

Patience is a virtue, especially in the field of IT. The more patient you are, the more progress you make. But as we wait, should we watch the time? How about ditching the watch in the next chapter? Intrigued yet?

CHAPTER VIII

Don't Wear a Watch!

"Lost time is never found again." - Benjamin Franklin

Welcome to the thought-provoking chapter titled "Don't Wear a Watch!" Before you raise your eyebrows, let me clarify: I'm not advising against literal wristwatches or suggesting a boycott of timekeeping devices; I know it is phones nowadays! Instead, I want to emphasize a vital aspect of a programmer's mindset: focusing on the task rather than constantly clock-watching.

In my years of programming and leading development teams, I've noticed some developers tend to check out as the end of the workday approaches mentally. They're like runners in a race whose only goal is to cross the finish line, even if it means leaving a trail of unfinished tasks in their wake.

Remember that programming isn't just about writing code; it's also about resolving issues, meeting project goals, and delivering a polished, fully functional product to the client. And to be brutally honest, sometimes this means burning the midnight oil or investing a slice of your weekend.

In any project, there will be times when fires need to be put out. The server might crash, the code could throw unexpected errors, or the client might want last-minute changes. When such emergencies arise, it's not the time to watch the clock but to step up, roll up your sleeves, and get to work.

Your value as a programmer is intrinsically tied to the responsibility you shoulder and your ability to navigate through unforeseen challenges. This doesn't mean you're expected to work round-the-clock or forego your personal life. However, it's about being prepared to pitch in when a critical situation arises and the team needs you.

So in this chapter, let's embark on a journey of understanding how our attitudes towards time and responsibility can shape our growth and success in the exciting realm of programming. Because being a great programmer isn't just about the code you write but also your commitment.

Alright, code wranglers, grab your keyboards and caffeinated beverages as we traverse through the time-space continuum in this whimsical chapter of our programming escapades, curiously labelled "Don't Wear a Watch!" No wristwatches were harmed in the making of this chapter.

Multitasking: Myth or Marvel?

Multitasking can sometimes seem like a superpower. You may envision yourself expertly bouncing between tasks, saving time, and achieving more. But consider a time when you attempted to juggle multiple tasks simultaneously.

Perhaps you were trying to savour a slice of pizza while engrossed in a blockbuster movie and simultaneously debugging a complicated code. More often than not, such scenarios culminate in a cold piece of pizza, a missed plot twist, and a bug still lurking in your code.

In reality, multitasking often boils down to rapidly switching attention between tasks, which can significantly degrade the quality of work. Research even suggests it can reduce productivity by as much as 40%.

This isn't to say you shouldn't eat pizza or watch movies, but focusing on one task at a time can often lead to better results when it comes to work.

To illustrate, imagine debugging a complex piece of software. Your attention is divided if you're also checking emails or scrolling through social media. You might overlook a minor detail in your code that causes a significant problem.

However, if you devote your full attention to the task, you'll likely spot and fix issues more quickly and efficiently.

So, while it might feel like you're achieving more by multitasking, it's often more practical to concentrate on one task at a time, complete it to the best of your ability, and then move on to the next. It's not about becoming a "human circus act", juggling countless tasks, but about performing each act precisely and excellently.

Procrastination - The Art of Keeping Up with Yesterday

Procrastination, often humorously referred to as "the art of keeping up with yesterday," is a familiar adversary in the workplace, particularly within the realm of programming. AIt's subtle enemy convinces us to delay tasks for seemingly logical reasons, leaving us playing catch-up instead of moving forward.

Let's imagine a scenario at the workplace to comprehend this better. Suppose you're a software developer, and you've been tasked with developing a new feature for your application.

The feature seems complex and daunting, and the prospect of starting it is slightly overwhelming. So, you tell yourself, "I'll clean up my codebase a bit first," or "I'll take some time to organize my emails before getting started." Hours or even days pass, and you have restructured your entire email inbox and cleaned up your workspace, but with no progress on the actual task.

Meanwhile, the deadline for the feature development looms closer and becomes a faint ghost haunting your tranquil moments.

That's procrastination in action - it subtly diverts your attention from the priority tasks to less urgent ones, causing delay and stress. Understanding this habit and taking steps to combat it are essential to achieving productivity and meeting deadlines.

Getting in the 'Flow' - When Time Travels Faster than Light

"Flow State" – the concept, first proposed by psychologist Mihaly Csikszentmihalyi, refers to a state of hyper-focus, where an individual becomes wholly absorbed in a task, losing track of time and even basic needs. It's like entering a different universe where your concentration is at its peak, and you are the master of your craft. As developers, achieving this state often leads to highly productive coding sessions.

Consider this real-life scenario for context. Jane, a software engineer, is working on a challenging new algorithm. As she delves into the problem, she starts to lose awareness of her surroundings.

The office noises fade into the background, and her attention is fully locked onto her screen. Hours pass by, but for Jane, it feels like mere minutes. She's so engrossed in her task that she doesn't even realize she skipped lunch. And guess what?

By the end of the day, not only has she crafted an elegant solution, but she's also managed to optimize it beyond the original requirement.

That, my friends, is 'Flow State' in action. While it cannot be switched on at will, recognizing its power and learning techniques to induce this state can significantly enhance your coding productivity.

The key lies in setting the right conditions, balancing challenge and skill level, and allowing oneself to be fully immersed in the task.

Embracing Your Inner 'Time Lord'

At the end of this journey, we're not literal Time Lords, defying the laws of physics (as much as Doctor Who fans might wish). However, we will be equipped with the necessary tools and knowledge to navigate the fast-paced vortex of programming. Our ultimate goal? To evolve you into a proficient programmer who can effectively juggle tasks, adhere to deadlines, and still clock out in time to enjoy that well-deserved break.

Imagine this scenario: When you notice the clock, you're coding away, managing a flurry of different tasks. It's five in the evening, but the day has just started. You've hit all your daily targets and still have time to spare for a quick game of ping-pong or to catch up with friends at happy hour. Sounds like a dream, right?

That's the promise of becoming a 'Time Lord' in programming. You can turn this dream into your everyday reality by mastering your control over time. So, ready to jump into the time vortex and come out on the other side as a proficient 'Time Lord'? Let's embark on this exciting journey with our fingers on the keyboard and our eyes on the clock!

Remember, time might be an abstract concept, but deadlines are concrete. And we wouldn't want those to become fossils in the history of your programming career, would we? So, let's get ready to take charge of time!

Congratulations! You've discovered the timelessness of coding. While your computer runs your algorithms, it's time to explore the untamed wilderness of creativity in the next chapter. Ready to paint your canvas with some binary colours?

CHAPTER IX

Embrace Your Creativity!

" "Coding is a creative process. An algorithm must be seen as a brush, with computer code its paint." - Kevlin Henney "

Welcome, fellow code connoisseurs, to a chapter that might raise eyebrows - "Embrace Your Creativity!"

Hold on a second! Before you bolt away, declaring, "I'm a programmer, not Picasso!" allow me to reassure you. We aren't about to plunge into digital design's complicated realms or artistic impressionism's nuances. What we're aiming for is to unveil the invisible layer of creativity that's integrated into every single line of code we craft.

Yes, you heard it right. Creativity isn't limited to artists or designers; it's also a vital component of programming.

I still remember when I first started my career. I used a standard colour palette of maroon, grey, and black for designing applications. The lack of variety in my designs drew a comment from my boss. He looked at me one day and said, "You don't seem to have any creative skills!"

Initially, I was taken aback. But over time, I realized that coding, just like painting, needs a splash of creativity. So, brace yourself as we dive into this intriguing endeavour to merge the worlds of coding and creativity. Who knows, you might discover your inner Picasso in the process!

Contrary to popular belief, programming is far from a mundane task that merely involves following strict logical structures and protocols. Instead, it's a blend of rational thinking and creative problem-solving that brings a unique melody to our digital symphony.

Consider this from my personal treasure trove of experiences. I was once part of a project discussion where we faced a peculiar problem. We required customers to input their router device ID while logging in to view their devices' reports. It sounds straightforward, right?

Well, not quite. You see, a router device ID is a unique alphanumeric string; the length and complexity could rival the plot of a Christopher Nolan movie.

23

Instead of turning this into an episode of 'Mission Impossible: Remember Your Router ID,' we decided to flex our creative muscles. But let's hold that thought right there, as I can see your anticipation is building. This story, among others, will unravel as we journey through the chapter.

Fast forward to a fateful project discussion. The task was simple: customers must input their router device ID to access device-specific reports. But a simple task rarely stays simple in the world of programming.

In this case, router device IDs were alphanumeric strings, comparable to the coordinates of a hidden treasure, complex and near impossible to remember. We could've handed this burden to the customers, but that seemed like a one-way ticket to Unhappy-Client-Ville.

Instead, we decided to get creative. We brainstormed solutions, each more outrageous than the last—one proposal involved carrier pigeons and Post-it notes. Thankfully, we settled on a less feathery approach.

We crafted an innovative solution after many caffeine-induced brainstorming sessions and rounds of passionate scribbling. We designed a system that allowed automatic detection and population of the router device ID for returning customers. And how did we achieve this? Simply by leveraging the power of QR Codes!

When customers returned, they would scan a QR Code on the device using their phone. Upon scanning, this would automatically trigger the opening of our application. The application then swiftly registers the device, bypassing any manual input from the customer.

This solution not only eased the process for the customer, reducing their burden of having to remember and manually input device IDs, but it also added a level of intelligence to our application. I

It showcased the elegance of combining creativity with technology - a blend crucial in the programming world. These subtle touches of ingenious creativity can elevate a good program into a great one.

And voila! It was - problem solved, all because of a pinch of creative thinking! This experience taught us an essential lesson that programming isn't merely about bulldozing through obstacles with technical prowess. It's about brainstorming, innovating, and occasionally, opting against more unconventional methods, like our feathered friend, the carrier pigeon.

This scenario perfectly demonstrates what I regard as creativity in programming. It's all about thinking out of the box, stepping into the customer's shoes, and asking, ' What is the simplest solution to this problem?' This approach mirrors the KISS (Keep It Simple, Stupid)

principle, a design rule that emphasizes simplicity over needless complexity.

Creativity isn't always about producing the most elegant or complex code in programming. Sometimes, it's about leveraging existing technologies, like QR codes, and integrating them innovatively to enhance user experience and productivity. It's about keeping the user at the heart of the solution and making their life easier, one line of code at a time.

Creativity and programming go together like coffee and late-night coding sessions. Now you've stirred up your creativity, it's time to face some pain for real gain. Ready to build some tech muscles?

CHAPTER X

No Gain Without the Pain!

""Success is stumbling from failure to failure with no loss of enthusiasm." - Winston Churchill"

Welcome aboard, brave programmers, to the adrenaline-pumping journey that we've cryptically named "No Gain Without the Pain!" Buckle up, for we're about to venture into the wild roller coaster ride that is the life of a programmer, where every challenging problem is a new ride and every solution a thrilling victory!

Picture this, fellow code-riders: you're in a project meeting. The air is thick with the buzz of an unresolved problem, a tricky beast that scoffs at your existing technological arsenal.

The team leader asks, "Who's ready to tackle this monster and learn new technologies?" How many hands go up?

From my experience, you could count them on the one hand, and you'd still have fingers left over for a spot of air guitar.

Now, imagine you're in that room. Would your hand be shooting up like a student who knows the answer in class?

If you just nodded enthusiastically, congratulations! You're already on the path to becoming a successful developer.

If you didn't, don't worry; we'll dive into why you should.

Being a programmer isn't just about solving problems but embracing them. It's about grinning in the face of a challenge and saying, "Bring it on!" You're not just a code monkey; you're a code gladiator, stepping into the arena every day, ready to wrestle with monstrous problems and emerge victorious.

So, without further ado, let's dive headfirst into the adventurous programming world, where every problem is an opportunity to grow and every failure a stepping stone to success!

When I joined a leading development company in the mid-2000s, they sought to establish an open-source development department. Although I had no experience setting up infrastructure like servers, version control, communication tools, or networking, I successfully managed the endeavour.

Today, that company boasts a team of over 100 developers working on open-source projects.

As a developer, you will encounter countless opportunities to learn new things and tackle tasks you've never attempted. These moments are where you can truly make a difference!

Even if the chances of failure are high, seize the opportunity. Trust me, the lessons you'll learn from such experiences will prove invaluable in your future endeavours.

The Fearless and the Risk-Averse

Do you remember the sinking feeling when your teacher picked you out to answer a tricky question in front of the class?

That's how some developers feel when faced with an unfamiliar problem or technology. And it's understandable. Stepping outside our comfort zone is scary, like wandering into a haunted house with nothing but a faulty flashlight.

But remember, every great developer has walked that path. They've plunged into the unknown, faced the proverbial boogeyman of unfamiliarity, and emerged stronger and smarter.

Let me share a story from my coding chronicles that demonstrates this.

The Jittery Journey into JavaScript

It was when I was comfortable with PHP, as cosy as a cat curled up on a warm laptop.

However, the winds of change were blowing, bringing with them a project that demanded knowledge of JavaScript, a language I had managed to steer clear of. I was at a crossroads, two clear paths in front of me: to shy away or to dive in.

Faced with this dilemma, I chose the latter. I was apprehensive but also thrilled by the challenge. After all, how bad could it be?

Those initial days were akin to navigating a maze with a blindfold. But gradually, I began to grasp the language's quirks and nuances. The curly braces and semi-colons, which initially seemed like cryptic hieroglyphs, started making sense. Slowly but surely, I was evolving, not just as a programmer, but as a problem solver.

The Triumph of Tenacity

So there I was, at the end of my JavaScript journey, standing victorious on the peak of Mount 'New Project.' I hadn't just cracked the project; I'd smashed it like a rockstar smashes their guitar after an electrifying concert. JavaScript had become a shiny new tool in my coding utility belt, ready for action whenever needed.

And you know what? Things got heated, and I mean React.js and Node.js hot. Was I prepared for it? Heck, no! But I did it, and the sense of accomplishment was sweeter than a fresh batch of chocolate chip cookies.

But let's not forget, the real gold wasn't just at the end of the rainbow, but it was the rainbow itself! It was all about the roller coaster ride - confronting my fear of the unknown, taking a leap of faith, and hugging the thrilling beast of learning. And what a ride it was!

So, strap in, fellow adventurers, for an exciting journey into the unpredictable and exhilarating realm of coding!

They say 'no pain, no gain', and you've proved it true by mastering the art of programming. But what's coding without some chatter? Let's add some words to our lines of code in the next chapter.

CHAPTER XI

It's All About Communication!

""Programming isn't about what you know; it's about what you can figure out." - Chris Pine"

Welcome, dear readers, to the lively chapter whimsically titled "It's All About Communication!" Or, as I like to call it, "How to stop sounding like a robot and start talking like a human."

In the tech realm, there's an age-old stereotype of programmers being no more expressive than a brick wall. Many believe developers are similar to sloths in non-coding activities, preferring to hang upside down in their coding tree, munching on the leaves of a juicy problem. At the same time, the world of communication goes on below.

While the blissful solitude of your coding tree can be appealing, you'll soon realise that these non-coding activities aren't optional extras; they're a part of the main course.

Whether drafting an eloquent email, standing up in a meeting and presenting like a TED speaker, or documenting your code in a way that doesn't require a decoder ring, it all boils down to communication. As you ascend the career ladder, you must master these skills to succeed.

But don't panic! This chapter'll explore why being a developer isn't just about speaking fluent Python or Java. It's about speaking fluent humans. It's about conveying your genius solutions in a language that stakeholders and customers understand and appreciate.

After all, what's the use of a brilliant solution if it's lost in translation?

So, let's embark on a journey to transform you from a coding sloth to a communication maestro, helping your brilliance shine in every aspect of your work.

Now, we must remember that as developers, we're not just typing away in a secluded corner of the world, but we're creating for an audience as diverse and global as the United Nations!

This means that your communication needs to be on point, my friends. An odd typo here or a quirky grammar mistake there might seem innocuous to you, but to your international customers, it might be as conspicuous as a pink elephant in a herd of grey.

And believe me; nothing crumbles your image faster in the eyes of your audience than a misplaced comma or a puzzling sentence construction. They might start wondering, "If they can't even get their English right, how can I trust them with my code?" Scary, right?

But don't worry; I'm not here to scare you off. Instead, let me introduce you to your new best friends - writing aids! These are fantastic tools like Grammarly, which don't just fix your spelling and grammar faster than you can say "syntax error" but also help you enhance your writing style. It's like having a private English tutor, minus the scary red pen marks on your work.

Plus, thanks to the magic of AI, these tools can even help you diversify your vocabulary. So, no more repeating the same word until it loses all meaning. You can easily find synonyms for overused or misspelt words, making your writing as varied as a programmer's coffee choices.

So, fellow code whisperers, it's time to step up your writing game. Use these tools, proofread your work, and watch as your credibility in the international arena skyrockets! Remember, your coding skills are the show's star, but your communication skills are the spotlight that makes the star shine.

You've proved yourself to be quite the conversationalist. However, communication is not just about talking; it's about working well with others. Ready to unlock the superpower of teamwork?

CHAPTER XII

Be a Great Team Player!

""A team is not a group of people who work together. A team is a group of people who trust each other." - Simon Sinek"

Ladies and gentlemen, start your engines, for you're about to dive headfirst into the grand raceway of teamwork in the programming world! This thrilling chapter, aptly named "Be a Great Team Player!" takes you into the intricate dynamics of working together in the coding pit stop.

Developers are not like wizards who work alone in a tower. They are more like a team of racecar drivers. Each has a task, like a part of a race track to drive on. Sometimes, they might feel like they're racing each other, but their main job is to work together to win the big race. That big race? It's the success of their project.

If you have dreams of victory laps in your developer career, you'll inevitably find yourself in a team, navigating the thrilling curves of coding projects. You'll need to master the art of changing tires in the pit stop of debugging, refuelling ideas in strategy meetings, and, most importantly, driving in sync with your teammates.

So, buckle up and get ready to embrace the fast-paced world of teamwork in programming. It's time to shift gears, hit the accelerator, and let's race towards becoming a top-tier team player in the coding universe. Let the race begin!

Becoming a great team player involves a few key principles. Firstly, it's important to understand your teammates genuinely. Not just what they say, but what they truly mean.

This requires active listening and the willingness to ask questions during discussions or fieldwork sessions. Such practices build trust among team members and ensure everyone comprehends the task.

Secondly, proactiveness and initiative are vital attributes of a great team player. Be willing to take on tasks and responsibilities beyond your designated role, showcasing your reliability and dedication to going the extra mile for the team's success.

Lastly, exceptional team players constantly seek ways to improve. They actively seek feedback and learn from their mistakes. This eagerness to grow demonstrates your commitment to being an integral part of a high-performing team.

Additionally, it's crucial to develop the skill of collaborative problem-solving. By exploring different approaches and encouraging diverse ideas, every team member can contribute valuable insights that pave the way for success.

Many people might think developers like to work alone, but that's not usually true. Most developers do their best work when they're part of a team. Sure, some can work perfectly well alone, especially if they are very experienced. But for most people, being part of a team is the best way to go.

Please don't misunderstand me. I'm not saying that you can't succeed in IT if you're an introverted person or prefer to work alone. Everyone is different, and there are many paths to success.

However, the focus of this book is on how to reach the very top in your career, and from my own experience, I believe that working as part of a team is a crucial skill for this, particularly in India. We are talking about what is most common, not the exceptions to the rule.

A pat on the back for being a splendid team player! But let's not stop at that. Let's take your interpersonal skills up a notch, shall we? Our next stop, 'People Skills: A Superpower!'

CHAPTER XIII

People Skills: A Superpower!

"Your most important skill in life is your ability to get along with people." - Robert Kiyosa"

In the Marvel Universe of life skills, there's a superpower that doesn't get the flashy spotlight it deserves, and that, my friends, is the magnificent world of people skills. Welcome to this action-packed chapter, "People Skills: A Superpower!" where we'll be suiting up to unleash the true power of human interaction.

Have you ever watched Spiderman swing across the city using his web? Just like how he moves easily from one building to another, people skills can help you interact smoothly with others at work and in your personal life.

Think of people skills like Spiderman's superpowers. Active listening is like Spiderman's super hearing – it lets you understand what others are saying. Being able to help people solve their disagreements is another critical skill. It's like being a superhero who helps people get along.

And don't forget to be patient with people different from you. This is a big part of having good people skills. If you can do this, you'll be able to work well in a team, encourage your co-workers, and even make your clients happy.

So, it's time to put on your superhero cape because we'll learn all about people skills. And remember, just like Spiderman says, "With great power comes great responsibility." This means it's important to understand and respect the people around you. Let's go!

We are all human beings collaborating with other human beings. Your ability to connect with others will bring you greater satisfaction and joy in your work. People skills are crucial not only for developers but for professionals in any field and in society at large.

As a developer, you will inevitably require help and guidance. Whether you manage a team, work as a CEO or CTO, or pursue other leadership roles, your success will hinge on your people skills.

The simplest solution to developing these skills is to cultivate empathy and avoid arrogance. Nurturing these qualities will naturally guide you in fostering positive relationships. We will delve deeper into this topic in future chapters.

In conclusion, dear reader, you have now discovered some essential ingredients for becoming the best programmer you can be. Remember the words of Steve Jobs, the visionary behind Apple:

"Everyone should learn how to program a computer because it teaches you how to think."

Let this quote serve as a constant reminder of the immense value programming holds, not just as a technical skill but as a pathway to sharpen your mind and expand your horizons.

Your charm is now your superpower, but are you ready to put your mindset into overdrive and decipher the 'Power of Code'? Come on; there's no looking back now!

CHAPTER XIV

The Power of Code: Nurturing the Developer's Mindset

"Your mindset matters. It affects everything - from the business and investment decisions you make, to the way you raise your children, to your stress levels and overall well-being." - Peter Diamandis

Welcome to a fantastic journey into the labyrinth of the mind! Our next adventure, "Developers Gone Wild - Unleashing Your Inner Leader," is about the magical 'developer mindset.'

We've journeyed far and wide across numerous chapters, uncovering the secrets of success in the coding realm. From the art of patience to the nuances of effective communication and teamwork, we've explored many facets of the multi-dimensional gem of a successful developer.

But hold onto your keyboards, dear readers, because we've yet to unveil the most enchanting piece of this puzzle, the one that can turn you from a mere code crafter into a programming prodigy. Drumroll, please... It's all about the Programmer Mindset!

This riveting chapter will dive into the fascinating transformation of a timid academic rabbit into a roaring corporate lion. Through this voyage, we'll unravel the significance of adopting a mindset that resonates with leadership, confidence, and the audacity to take risks.

Join me as we venture into the enigmatic territories of the developer's mind, unveiling the crucial elements that make for a genuinely exceptional programmer. After all, it's not just about slinging code; it's about the magic you can create with the right mindset.

Developers are often compared to soldiers. Rightfully so! Attitude and mindset hold the key to your ranks. If you fancy being a general, you've got to act like one—decisive, confident, a risk-taker.

So, for all the coding aspirants out there, this chapter is for you. Developer mindset—it's your invisible cape! Just like your muscles, the more you exercise it, the stronger it becomes.

My first job as a developer barely paid the bills. Heck, even my peers made more. But in just two years, I was out-earning them all. Yes, you heard it right!

Now, this wasn't because my peers lacked technical finesse. Some coded way better than I ever could. But what tilted the scale in my favour? The secret sauce was my mindset and my approach. Seeing value in teamwork and embracing the learning curve—that's what fast-tracked my journey.

It isn't always about breaking into the field in the corporate race. It's about sporting the right mindset and honing your skills. As programmers, we might not need the persuasion skills of a marketer or the negotiation tactics of a salesperson. But the 'developer mindset'? Oh, that's our Holy Grail.

So, as we tread further, let's take a leaf from Steve Jobs' book: "Stay hungry, stay foolish." Unleash your inner leader and see how you transform from a programmer to a maestro!

Remember that programmer who raced with your team and then got lost in the woods of codes? Or, perhaps, your old pal from college who aced all the programming tests yet keeps bouncing from job to job? Sounds familiar? Well, you, my friend, are about to dive into a goldmine of enlightenment.

When it comes to coding, it's not the knowledge or the skillset that makes you stand tall among the crowd. Sure, they are essential, but what truly separates the wheat from the chaff is 'The Developer Mindset.' A mindset that goes beyond knowing the language or solving a problem; it's about seeing the bigger picture, embracing failures, and having the perseverance to march ahead.

So, let's cut to the chase. The developer's mindset, you ask?

The secret sauce turns a good programmer into a great one! This mindset, much like muscle, gets stronger with exercise. And what's the workout, you ask? It's constantly learning, evolving, and breaking out of your shell.

Like in Game of Thrones, you don't need to birth dragons or control the undead to succeed. You need to cultivate the 'developer's mindset.' As we proceed, we'll unravel the mysteries of this mindset, so buckle up!

In the wise words of Albert Einstein, "Once you stop learning, you start dying." So gear up, dear reader. Unleash your inner programming genius and embrace the journey of becoming an exceptional developer!

The developer's mindset is a unique mental model that enables one to face challenges head-on, adapt to changing circumstances, and consistently learn new things. It's an attitude that turns problems into puzzles and sees failure as a stepping stone rather than a dead end.

When you adopt a developer's mindset, problems become opportunities. You begin to look forward to troubleshooting because it allows you to flex your problem-solving muscles.

You begin to enjoy the thrill of finding a bug because it's a chance to learn something new. When you think like a developer, you don't run from challenges; you embrace them.

Now, let's consider a real-life example of this. Imagine you're a developer working on a web app and suddenly hit a roadblock. An unexpected bug has appeared, causing chaos in the codebase. The traditional reaction might be feeling frustrated, stressed, and perhaps even slightly panicky. But with a developer's mindset, the response is different.

You see this bug as an opportunity to learn, a puzzle waiting to be solved, and you get to work. You enjoy the process of debugging and learning, and eventually, you emerge victorious, having gained new insights and experiences.

A developer's mindset also includes a hunger for learning. Technologies and programming languages are constantly evolving, and what's considered cutting-edge today might be old news tomorrow. Hence, a true developer is always learning, curious, and ready to adapt.

Finally, a developer with the right mindset knows that success doesn't come overnight. It comes with consistent hard work, resilience, and the courage to continue even when things get tough.

A great developer understands that every failure is a lesson, every bug is an opportunity, and every piece of code is a stepping stone towards success.

So, fellow code warriors, let's embark on this journey towards cultivating a powerful developer mindset! Remember, it's not the strength of the code that matters but the power of the coder behind it.

The Power of Code: Nurturing the Developer's Mindset" Kudos! You've genuinely nurtured the developer's mindset. Next, let's dive deep and explore some unorthodox pathways into the coding pool. Do you think you can swim with the sharks? There's only one way to find out!

CHAPTER XV

Unorthodox Pathways – Leaping into the Coding Pool

""Fearlessness is not the absence of fear. It's the mastery of fear. It's about getting up one more time than we fall down." - Arianna Huffington"

Unconventional paths have always intrigued me. The thought of following the crowd, the conventional norms, was never my cup of tea. So, when I decided to jump into the programming pool with a master's in chemistry and an MBA in Marketing under my belt, it wasn't a surprise to me. To many, it was a shock, a surprise, a confusion. It was the step I needed to take to be myself.

Now, you must be wondering why such a drastic switch. It's simple, really. It was my passion. Coding, solving problems, creating something out of nothing excited me, thrilled me, and satisfied me in ways words fail to describe. The world of zeros and ones, where logic reigns supreme, was where I found my solace and joy.

Given my academic background, the decision to steer my career towards programming wasn't the easiest. Back then, resources were limited, with no Google or online courses to rely upon. The ocean of knowledge was vast, and I was a mere sailboat with a tiny compass, trying to navigate through the unknown, undeterred by the uncertainties.

When I started my journey, many raised their eyebrows. Some even laughed. But I knew one thing - when you find your passion, you should embrace it wholeheartedly.

I knew the satisfaction that ensued every time I solved a problem, every time a line of code ran smoothly. I knew the thrill of creating something that had the potential to influence lives, to bring about a difference. And above all, I knew the joy of working on something I loved.

It was time to shake things up. It was time to surprise everyone.

As we have explored the qualities of a successful programmer and whether a career in programming is the right fit for you, let us now dive into how you can begin your journey in IT.

Formal computer or programming education was limited in the past, and physical classrooms were the primary option. However, in today's digital era, you can forge a career in programming without formal education. While pursuing a degree in computer engineering may be necessary for scientific or innovative roles, building a successful career in programming does not require such formal education. Many large corporations now prioritize skills and practical experience over degrees when hiring programmers or coders.

During my time, computer education was not widely available, and my team had little formal programming education. Computers emerged during my college years, and today, computer education starts early in schools, equipping students with the foundational knowledge needed to begin their journey in IT.

With numerous options available, you can choose a path that aligns with your interests and objectives. Whether you aspire to be a web developer, a mobile app developer, a desktop application programmer, or an AI/ML programmer, your choice should be driven by passion, commercial viability, or a combination of both.

Conduct thorough research on the future demand, growth, and potential in your chosen field to make an informed decision.

When embarking on your IT career, you have a plethora of channels to explore, depending on your age, career goals, and financial situation.

While fast-track and costly courses promise high-paying IT jobs in a short time, I encourage a different approach based on my own experience. Start by learning the basics from freely available resources such as YouTube tutorials, Udemy courses, or online forums.

Here's my recommended path to success:

- Master the basics and create a "Hello World" project to get started.
- Replicate projects from tutorials, following step-by-step instructions to build your skills.
- Define small problems or case studies for your own projects to deepen your understanding.
- Develop small projects that address the identified problems, honing your coding abilities.
- Create a GitHub account to showcase and store your projects, building a portfolio.

- Deploy your projects in a way that allows you to present and demonstrate your work effectively.
- Repeat these steps, gradually tackling more complex problems to sharpen your programming prowess.

By following this path, you will gain valuable experience in problem-solving, solution planning, code simplicity and reusability, testing, debugging, and project deployment.

Additionally, with the advent of AI and tools like ChatGPT, starting a programming career has become even more accessible. I have authored a couple of books on this subject, specifically focusing on how AI tools can accelerate your journey into programming. You can find these books on popular platforms such as Amazon, where I share practical insights and techniques to jumpstart your programming career using AI-powered tools.

As we embark on this enlightening journey together, armed with knowledge, humor, and a touch of wit, let me leave you with a quote that resonates with the challenges and triumphs of programming:

"Programming is like writing a book. Except when you misspell a word, the entire universe gets upset." - Unknown

You've certainly taken a leap of faith into the vast coding pool. Are you ready to suit up for success? The interview room is just around the corner. A little nerve-racking? Absolutely! But remember, fortune favors the brave!

CHAPTER XVI

Suit Up For Success: Interviews and Resumes Unmasked

""You never get a second chance to make a first impression." Oscar Wilde,"

When it comes to programming, these words couldn't ring truer. In this tech-driven world where code is the common language, your resume and how you perform in an interview are your first impressions, your key to unlocking the door of opportunities.

In previous chapters, we've hacked into the mind of a programmer and discovered what makes them tick. Now that you're primed and ready to jump into the coding arena, it's time to tackle the next big bosses – job interviews and crafting an irresistible resume.

But fear not, intrepid coder! These seemingly daunting tasks are not as horrifying as a bug in your code at 2 AM. Like a well-written code, they require a dash of logic, a pinch of creativity, and heaps of understanding of the end user – in this case, your potential employer.

So buckle up and let's dive into the nitty-gritty of acing your interview and scripting the perfect resume.

"In the iconic words of William Shakespeare, 'All the world's a stage, and all the men and women merely players.' This quote brings back memories of my own journey and reminds me that everyone plays a unique role, and it is up to us to decide what that will be.

In previous chapters, we discussed what qualities make a successful programmer and how you can start your journey into programming. We're assuming that you've soaked in all that information and are ready to kickstart your career in programming.

Now, let's discuss the next crucial step—preparing for your interview and building a compelling resume.

Great job! You're ready to conquer any interview room. But let's pause for a moment. Your resume is your story; is it grand enough?

CHAPTER XVII

Showcasing Your Grand Odyssey: The Resume Chronicles

""The secret of getting ahead is getting started." - Mark Twain"

Crafting your resume is like telling your professional story to the world. It's the perfect chance to show everyone who you are, what you've done, and what you can do in the future. It's like your key to open the door of job opportunities. Now, let's start telling your story in a way that will leave a big impression!

In the programming world, there are many job opportunities and a lot of competition. That's why having a good resume is so important. Your resume speaks for you, telling future employers what you can do even before you meet them in an interview.

The tricky part is figuring out how to show off your skills without overloading your resume with information.

I've learned much about writing resumes from my experiences and looking at many other resumes. Most importantly, I realized that a simple, focused resume is the best. When I started, I tried to put every skill I had on my resume. But later, I learned that it's not about how much you put on your resume but the quality of what you put on it.

Albert Einstein, a famous scientist, once said, "If you can't explain it simply, you don't understand it well enough." This is really true for resumes too. You shouldn't just list all your skills and experiences. You should carefully pick the most important and impressive ones to share.

In this chapter, we'll learn how to write a good resume. We'll learn what makes a resume stand out and grab the attention of people hiring for jobs. We'll discuss how to show off your skills, experiences, and unique qualities well.

Whether you're a professional looking for a new job or a new graduate starting, these tips will help you write a resume that will get noticed and make people interested in you.

I also want to mention LinkedIn. This website allows you to make a profile that acts like a modern resume. While it's beyond the scope of this book to tell you everything about using LinkedIn, I suggest you spend some time learning how to use it for your job search. A good LinkedIn profile can be a potent tool.

Here are some tips for a good LinkedIn profile:

1. Have a professional photo: This gives an excellent first impression.
2. Write a clear summary: This is like your elevator pitch. It should tell people who you are and what you can do.
3. List your skills: Like on your resume, your LinkedIn profile should show off your skills.
4. Share your experiences: Talk about your past jobs or projects. This gives people a better idea of what you can do.
5. Connect with others: LinkedIn is a social network. The more people you connect with, the more opportunities you might find.

Remember, your LinkedIn profile is like a living, breathing resume. Keep it updated and make it the best it can be!

During my early years in the industry, I reviewed dozens of resumes for Video Streaming Engineers. What struck me was how a fresher's resume was more detailed than a seasoned professional's. A common misconception is that including more skills improves your chances. However, that might not always be the case.

Once, a fellow junior developer and I applied for the same position in another company. We both got the interview call, but in the end, he was the one who landed the job. He later shared that instead of listing all his skills, he focused on those relevant to the job, making his resume crisp and impactful.

There was an exciting incident at one of the companies I worked at. A senior PHP developer who had left our company was discovered to have submitted a fake salary receipt and appointment letter with forged signatures. This taught me the gravity of being honest, not just in interviews but in every professional dealing.

Building your resume is much like constructing a building. You want it to stand tall and distinguished among countless others. A sturdy foundation (honesty), suitable materials (relevant skills), and pleasing aesthetics (presentation) are crucial. I remember using websites offering resume-building templates and tools like Grammarly to ensure my resume was error-free.

When I was crafting my resume, my mentor gave me some invaluable advice. He said, 'Your resume should be a clear reflection of you. Keep it simple, concise, and honest.' This advice has stuck with me and helped me throughout my career.

Listing skills that you're proficient in and categorizing them based on expertise not only shows your range but also tells your potential employer where your strengths lie. Highlight the domains you have experience in, showcase the challenging projects, and explain their significance. Remember, the little details can make a huge difference.

A crucial aspect of crafting an effective resume is getting feedback from others. Having a fresh pair of eyes look at your work is always beneficial. I made it a habit to update my resume and regularly seek feedback from my mentors.

As a seasoned professional, I've learned that it's not the length but the substance of the resume that matters. Highlighting my experience, categorizing my skills based on my expertise, and keeping it simple yet impactful has been my mantra. And yes, honesty, even on paper, matters a lot. Companies often conduct background checks, and a lie can lead to unfortunate consequences.

As we conclude our journey through the complex landscape of resume building, remember that your resume is your story. It's a chronicle of your grand odyssey intended to pique potential employers' curiosity. But it's just the beginning. It sets the stage for the next big challenge – interviews.

What questions should you anticipate? How should you respond to them? What strategies should you use to portray your skills effectively during an interview?

We will dive into these exciting topics in our next chapter, 'Cracking the Code: The Decoding of Interviews.' The journey continues, and so does your growth. Are you ready to decode the mystery of interviews?

CHAPTER XVIII

Cracking the Code: The Decoding of Interviews

"Be yourself; everyone else is already taken." - Oscar Wilde,

So, you've crafted your resume, a remarkable narrative of your professional odyssey, and it's garnered you a spot in the final battleground. Now, it's showtime!

The interview is the proverbial dance where you twirl and leap, demonstrating your skills, experiences, and, most importantly, your unique self. It's an intimate tango with potential employers, a chance to convince them that you are the missing puzzle piece they've been seeking. So, dust off that nervousness and stride into the spotlight; it's time to shine!

But interviews can be nerve-wracking. The pressure to perform and impress can sometimes overshadow the true purpose of this interaction. It's not just about providing the correct answers; it's about presenting your authentic self and demonstrating your potential to contribute to the company's success.

As I reflect on my interview experiences, I realize that technical knowledge is just one piece of the puzzle. Yes, having a solid foundation in your field is essential, but equally crucial is your ability to communicate effectively, display problem-solving skills, and showcase your enthusiasm for learning and growth.

I remember one particular interview where I encountered a question that stumped me. It was a programming problem I hadn't met before, and I felt a momentary panic. However, instead of trying to fake my way through it, I took a deep breath and admitted that I didn't know the answer. To my surprise, the interviewer appreciated my honesty and used it as an opportunity to gauge my problem-solving approach and willingness to learn.

This experience taught me the value of authenticity in interviews. It's not about pretending to know everything; it's about being genuine, humble, and open to new challenges. Employers are not just looking for a perfect candidate; they want someone willing to grow, adapt, and bring their unique perspective.

In this chapter, we will explore the art of interviews and explore strategies that will help you shine during this crucial stage of the hiring process. From preparation and mindset to effective communication and showcasing your potential, we will provide you with valuable insights and practical tips based on personal experiences and industry best practices.

Remember, an interview is not a test of your worth; it's an opportunity to demonstrate your true potential. So, embrace authenticity, confidently approach interviews, and let your genuine self shine through.

Steve Jobs once said, "Your work will fill a large part of your life, and the only way to be truly satisfied is to do what you believe is great work. And the only way to do great work is to love what you do."

Let's embark on this journey together and master the art of interviews to unlock the door to your dream career.

Welcome to the world of interviews - where authenticity meets opportunity.

This is your chance to show them the 'real' you. This is your stage. I remember my first interview clearly. I was brimming with nervous energy, rehearsing the answers in my mind, hoping to impress the interviewer with my knowledge. But I soon realized that an interview is more than just a test of your technical skills.

One of my cherished interview experiences involved a question I couldn't answer. It was a tricky programming problem that I hadn't come across before. I admitted that I didn't know the answer. Instead of looking at it as a failure, the interviewer appreciated my honesty, and we discussed other things I was confident about.

The process reminded me that honesty is equally valuable in an interview as technical expertise. Even though you might not know everything, demonstrating the willingness to learn and being honest about your abilities can leave a lasting impression.

Interviews are your stage. It's where you showcase your talent and skills. I've walked into many interviews during my career, and I've learned that it's okay to say "I don't know" when you genuinely don't know something. I've observed that interviewers appreciate honesty over a fumbled answer.

One thing I noticed is that interviewers always appreciated my positive outlook. A smile goes a long way. It reflects your attitude and ability to handle situations positively, indicating your potential as a team player.

Answering technical questions was always a challenge for me initially. But with time, I realized the trick was to provide confident explanations with real-life examples. For instance, when asked about file validation, I would delve deeper into user needs, future improvements, and the system's configuration instead of a textbook answer about size and type.

The interview dress code can vary greatly, but my rule of thumb has always been to aim for intelligent and professional. Remember, you're not only demonstrating your technical abilities but also your communication skills, especially if you're interviewing for roles involving international interaction.

Finally, doing your homework about the company and the job profile is important. Analyze the market and understand your worth. Playing salary negotiation gambles based on what your friends earn might seem tempting, but remember, it rarely works. Always base your negotiation on your skills, experience, and industry standard.

As we conclude our exploration of interview strategies and decoding techniques, remember that every interview is a new opportunity to demonstrate your authentic self.

You've learned the skills, practised the techniques, and now you're ready to shine. But where does this path lead us next? What comes after cracking the interview code?

As it turns out, a labyrinth lies ahead, one that involves perfecting resumes, interviews, and skill exhibitions. In our next chapter, 'Navigating the Labyrinth: Perfecting Resumes, Interviews, and Skill Exhibition,' we will delve deeper into these intertwined aspects.

We'll explore how AI tools and ChatGPT can become your ally in this labyrinth, providing guidance and resources to refine your professional journey further. So, are you ready to navigate this labyrinth with AI as your compass?

CHAPTER XIX

Navigating the Labyrinth: Perfecting Resumes, Interviews, and Skill Exhibition

"'The most common way people give up their power is by thinking they don't have any.' - Alice Walker."

Alice Walker wisely said in her book, The Color Purple, "The most common way people give up their power is by thinking they don't have any." Regarding your IT career progression, this quote strikes a chord that reverberates through the grand halls of resume tailoring, interview acumen, and skill flaunting.

In this chapter, "Navigating the Labyrinth: Perfecting Resumes, Interviews, and Skill Exhibition", we will crack the enigmatic code of professional self-presentation. Because just as a book is often judged by its cover, your potential employer will most likely make the first impression of you based on your resume and interview performance.

So let's dive in! Let's arm ourselves with the best practices, tips, and tricks that can turn you from being just another face in the crowd to the star of the show in the eyes of your dream employer. Because remember, in this labyrinth of career progression, you're not without power—you need to know how to wield it effectively.

Resumes are your first opportunity to showcase your skills and experiences. With the help of AI tools, such as ChatGPT, you can generate well-crafted resume content and format it effectively. These tools provide prompts and suggestions, helping you highlight your strengths and tailor your resume to specific job requirements. Let's consider an example:

Prompt: "Describe your experience in project management."

AI-generated response: "With my strong project management skills, I have successfully led cross-functional teams and delivered complex projects within tight deadlines. I effectively utilize agile methodologies to ensure efficient project execution and foster collaboration among team members. One notable project I managed was implementing a new CRM system, resulting in a 20% increase in customer satisfaction."

By utilizing AI tools, you can create impactful resume content that showcases your expertise and accomplishments in a concise yet comprehensive manner.

Moving on to the interview process, AI tools can assist you in preparing for common interview questions and formulating effective responses. These tools can generate sample interview questions based on your chosen technology or industry, allowing you to practice your answers and gain confidence.

Let's see an example:

• • •

Prompt: "Describe a challenging situation you encountered during a project and how you resolved it."

• • •

"AI-generated response: "During a software development project, we faced a critical resource shortage due to unforeseen circumstances. To address this challenge, I proactively communicated with team members, redistributed tasks, and ensured clear priorities were established. By fostering a collaborative environment and implementing efficient task management strategies, we successfully navigated the crisis and delivered the project on time."
"

Real-life examples also play a significant role in showcasing your skills and experiences. When discussing your projects or accomplishments, provide specific details and outcomes. For instance:

"In my previous role, I implemented an automated testing framework that reduced the testing time by 50% and significantly improved the overall software quality."

Finally, adapt your communication style and language to suit the interview setting. If you are interviewing for a company with an international clientele, effective English communication skills are crucial. However, for many IT positions, fluency in the native language is often sufficient, especially for entry-level roles.

Here are some references you can consider:

- ChatGPT by OpenAI: https://www.openai.com/research/chatgpt/
- Grammarly: https://www.grammarly.com/
- Canva: https://www.canva.com/
- Novoresume: https://novoresume.com/
- Resume.com: https://www.resume.com/
- ResumeGenius: https://resumegenius.com/

These platforms offer AI-powered writing assistance, professional resume templates, and editing tools to help you create impressive resumes. They can streamline the resume writing process and ensure grammatical accuracy and visual appeal.

Additionally, consider exploring online career development platforms like LinkedIn Learning or Udemy, which provide courses on resume writing, interview skills, and professional development.

By referring to these resources, you can access valuable tools and platforms that enhance your resume writing abilities, improve your interview preparation, and boost your chances of success in the IT industry.

Remember, these references are provided as suggestions, and it's always advisable to thoroughly research and choose the platforms that best suit your needs and preferences.

To summarize, mastering the resume writing and interview process involves utilizing AI tools to enhance your resume content, practising interview responses, and effectively showcasing your skills and experiences. You can present yourself as a confident and qualified candidate by incorporating real-life examples and adapting your communication style.

Navigating the labyrinth was not as challenging as you thought. You've survived the trials and are ready for your first love. No, not that kind of love! Your first job. Ready to handle this crucial relationship?

CHAPTER XX

Dating with First Love – How to Handle Your Crucial First Job

""Success is not the key to happiness. Happiness is the key to success. If you love what you are doing, you will be successful." - Albert Schweitzer."

In the words of Chetan Bhagat, one of India's most influential writers, from his book Five Point Someone, "Life is not to be taken seriously, as we are really temporary here. We are like a pre-paid card with limited validity. If we are lucky, we may last another 50 years. And 50 years is just 2,500 weekends.

Do we really need to get so worked up? It's ok, bunk a few classes, goof up a few interviews, fall in love." This perspective encapsulates the essence of what your first job can feel like, filled with new experiences, mistakes, learnings, and perhaps a bit of love in the form of your newfound passion.

Your first job is akin to dating your first love, filled with nervous excitement, the desire to make a good impression, and the ambition to make it work. It is the beginning of a journey that will shape your career, cultivate your skills, and define your professional identity.

This experience holds the power to lay the foundation of your career path. Therefore, as you step into this new phase, it's crucial to approach it with enthusiasm, curiosity, and an open mind. It's an unparalleled opportunity for learning and growth. While your education has provided you with a solid theoretical knowledge foundation, the practical experience from your first job will truly mould your abilities as a professional.

In this chapter, "Dating with First Love - How to Handle Your Crucial First Job", we will explore the labyrinth of experiences that await you in your first job. We will discuss how to navigate the challenges, identify the activities to focus on, learn what to avoid, and how to prepare for future career transitions.

Drawn from my own experiences and the wisdom of countless other professionals who have been through this journey, I hope this guide will serve as a helpful companion as you navigate the thrilling, challenging, and fulfilling journey of your first job.

As you begin your first job, it's essential to approach it with a sense of enthusiasm and curiosity. Treat it as an opportunity to learn and grow. Remember, you may have acquired theoretical knowledge through your education, but practical experience is what truly shapes your skills as a programmer.

One crucial aspect of your first job is to learn the company's ropes and understand its culture. Take the time to observe and listen to your colleagues, especially those who have been with the company for a while. They can provide valuable insights and guidance as you navigate your role. Building relationships and seeking organizational mentors will accelerate your learning and growth.

Let's dive into a personal story to illustrate the importance of handling your first job with care. I was eager to prove myself and make a positive impression during my early days at IBM, one of the world's leading software development companies. However, I quickly realized that rushing to showcase my abilities without fully understanding the work environment could backfire.

One day, I encountered a challenging coding task and thought I had the perfect solution. Excitedly, I presented my idea to the team, only to discover that my approach overlooked critical considerations. It was a humbling experience that taught me the importance of seeking guidance, understanding the project requirements thoroughly, and collaborating with others before proposing solutions.

Learning from my mistake, I became more mindful of the knowledge and experience present within the team. I started to embrace a collaborative approach, actively seeking feedback and incorporating the expertise of my colleagues into my work. This not only improved the quality of my output but also fostered a sense of camaraderie within the team.

On your first job, it's crucial to balance showcasing your skills and being receptive to the expertise of others. Avoid showing off or imposing your ideas without understanding the larger context. Embrace the opportunity to learn from your peers and use their insights to refine your skills.

As a programmer, you'll encounter various activities on your first job. Each task contributes to your growth, from coding and debugging to testing and documentation. While focusing on your primary responsibilities is essential, don't shy away from exploring beyond your comfort zone.

Volunteer for additional projects seek opportunities to collaborate with different teams, and embrace challenges that stretch your abilities.

Maintaining a positive attitude and a growth mindset is crucial. Remember, mistakes are inevitable, especially early in your career. Embrace them as learning opportunities and use them to refine your skills. Be open to feedback and continuously seek ways to improve.

Throughout my career, I have had the privilege of working at IBM and with several other reputable software development companies, both large and small. Each experience taught me valuable lessons and helped shape my professional journey.

Now, let's delve into some practical advice for handling your first job:

1. Embrace a learning mindset: Your first job is a unique opportunity to absorb knowledge and gain practical experience. Be eager to learn, and don't hesitate to ask questions.

1. Build relationships: Networking is crucial in any profession. Connect with colleagues, attend company events, and seek mentorship opportunities to foster your growth.

3. Seek guidance: Don't be afraid to seek advice from experienced team members or mentors. They can provide valuable insights.

4. And guidance as you navigate the challenges of your first job. Their wisdom and experience can help you avoid common pitfalls and accelerate learning.

5. Communicate effectively: Effective communication is vital in any professional setting. Be clear, concise, and respectful in your interactions with colleagues and superiors. Listen actively and contribute meaningfully to discussions.

6. Embrace teamwork: Collaboration is a fundamental aspect of software development. Embrace teamwork and actively contribute to group projects. Learn from your colleagues and offer your support when needed.

7. Take ownership: Demonstrate your commitment and dedication by taking ownership of your tasks and responsibilities. Be proactive in identifying problems, proposing solutions, and delivering high-quality work.

8. Embrace feedback: Feedback is invaluable for personal and professional growth. Be open to receiving feedback from your peers and superiors. Use it as an opportunity to improve and refine your skills.

9. Manage your time effectively: Time management is crucial in a fast-paced work environment. Prioritize your tasks, set realistic deadlines, and balance quality and efficiency in your work.

10. Stay updated: The technology landscape is ever-evolving, and it's essential to stay updated with the latest trends and advancements in programming. Allocate time to continuous learning and professional development.

11. Maintain a positive attitude: Your attitude and mindset play a significant role in your success. Approach challenges with optimism, resilience, and a willingness to learn from setbacks.

> *"Now, let's inject a little humour into the chapter with a programming joke:"*

• • •

Why do programmers prefer dark mode? Because it's easier on the syntax!

• • •

All jokes aside, the lessons you learn during your first job will serve as the building blocks for your future career transitions. Take the time to reflect on your experiences, identify improvement areas, and set professional development goals. Seek out training opportunities, attend conferences or webinars, and explore certifications that align with your career aspirations.

Remember, your first job is not just about acquiring technical skills. It's about developing a professional mindset, building solid relationships, and understanding the dynamics of the industry. Embrace the challenges, cherish the victories, and let each experience shape you into a well-rounded and successful programmer.

In conclusion, your first job is a significant milestone in your programming journey. Approach it with enthusiasm, curiosity, and a willingness to learn. Embrace the lessons, seek guidance from experienced professionals, and make meaningful contributions to your team. With the right mindset and dedication, your first job will lay the groundwork for a fulfilling and prosperous career in the world of programming.

Wow, you're now a seasoned pro in handling your first job! But, remember, every career has its crossroads. The real challenge lies in making the right decisions. Ready to cross the road with me?

CHAPTER XXI

Career Crossroads: Navigating Crucial Decisions

""Life has many ways of testing a person's will, either by having nothing happen at all or by having everything happen all at once." - Paulo Coelho,"

In Paulo Coelho's renowned novel, "The Alchemist," he penned, "It's the possibility of having a dream come true that makes life interesting." In the landscape of our careers, dreams often translate into finding the right job, the right team, or the right company that aligns with our aspirations and values.

The decision to move on from your first job to explore new opportunities can often feel as monumental as the decision to get married. It's a commitment, a pledge to devote your time, energy, and skills to a new environment and a new team.

I distinctly recall the first time I decided to leave my first job, lured by the allure of working for a multinational giant like IBM. The promise of higher pay, the prestige that came with the brand name, the opportunity to work on large-scale projects - it all seemed incredibly appealing. But, as I soon discovered, all that glitters is not gold. A few months into the job, I realized that I hadn't given due thought to one crucial aspect: would I enjoy the work I was doing there?

In this chapter titled "Getting Married - The Most Important Decision of Your Career," we will delve into the importance of making informed career decisions. We'll discuss how to identify the right opportunities, the significance of aligning your career path with your passions, and the art of gracefully transitioning from one job to the next.

Just like getting married, choosing your next career move should involve careful thought, consideration, and introspection. I hope to arm you with the insights and strategies that will help you navigate this vital decision confidently and wisely.

As we journey through this chapter together, remember that your career is a marathon, not a sprint, and every decision you make is a stepping stone to your professional fulfilment.

Much like tying the knot in matrimony, bidding farewell to your first job and venturing into the wild unknown of new professional opportunities can be a thrilling yet nerve-wracking experience. In the sea of career choices, finding "The One" (job, that is) may seem like a daunting task. Fear not, for I am here to guide you through this exciting journey, sharing my own experiences and invaluable lessons learned along the way.

In this chapter, we'll explore when to leave your first job, how to identify your goals and prospects, and the types of jobs you should consider. But before we dive into the nitty-gritty, let's start with some soul-searching questions that you should ask yourself before embarking on this life-changing journey.

Question 1 AM I truly ready for a change?

Contemplate whether you have genuinely outgrown your current job or are experiencing a temporary slump. Consider your growth, learning opportunities, and job satisfaction. If you're consistently feeling unchallenged or unfulfilled, it may be time for a change.

Example: I realized that I had reached a plateau in my first job, and there were no further growth opportunities. This realization prompted me to seek a new challenge.

Question 2: What are my long-term career goals?

Reflect on your aspirations and how a new job could help you achieve them. Identify the skills you need to acquire, the experience you want to gain, and the type of work environment that best suits your ambitions.

Example: In my case, I failed to assess how my role at IBM aligned with my long-term career goals. The allure of a prestigious company and a higher salary overshadowed my true passion and interests.

Question 3: Have I thoroughly researched potential employers?

Before making a move, research prospective companies, their work culture, and the roles they offer. Speak to current or former employees to get a genuine understanding of the organization.

Example: If I had spoken to IBM employees before accepting the offer, I would have gained insights into the job's day-to-day responsibilities and whether it aligned with my interests.

In conclusion, remember that the decision to leave your first job and pursue new opportunities is a significant milestone in your career journey. Approach this decision with careful consideration, introspection, and a clear understanding of your goals. And above all, always follow your heart because when it comes to your career, true love (for your job) conquers all!

As we draw to a close on our exploration of career crossroads and the navigation of crucial decisions, remember that these crossroads are indeed opportunities for growth and transformation.

You've learned how to weigh your options, seek guidance, and ultimately, trust your instincts. But what happens once you've made these decisions? How do you take control of your professional journey and steer it in the direction of your choosing?

This is the exciting journey we embark upon in the next chapter, 'The Driver Seat - How to Start Controlling Your Professional Journey.' We will delve into the skills, mindsets, and strategies you need to take the wheel of your career. Are you ready to switch gears and jump into the driver's seat?

CHAPTER XXII

The Driver Seat – How to Start Controlling Your Professional Journey

""You must be the change you wish to see in the world" - Mahatma Gandhi"

In the words of the great Mahatma Gandhi, "You must be the change you wish to see in the world." This quote rings particularly true when steering the wheel of your professional journey. A successful career isn't just about being in the right place at the right time and making informed choices, trusting your instincts, and embracing changes with grace.

Taking you back to my early career days, I recall a pivotal moment when I found myself at a crossroads, faced with the choice between ASP.NET and PHP. At the time, ASP.NET was the belle of the ball, a tried and tested staple in the programming world. On the other hand, PHP was the new kid on the block, full of potential but lacking the reputation and reliability that ASP.NET had earned.

The choice was clear for many – stick with the established and proven ASP.NET. However, I was drawn towards PHP, enchanted by its promise of revolutionizing web development. Choosing PHP over ASP.NET felt akin to going against the tide, a rebel challenging the status quo. Yet, much like a moth to a flame, I couldn't resist the pull towards PHP.

In this chapter, "The Driver Seat - Taking Control of Your Professional Journey," we will explore the importance of making choices in your career that resonates with your passions, even if they diverge from the conventional path. We will delve into proactively shaping your career narrative, embracing changes, and honing your skills to adapt to the evolving tech landscape.

As we journey together, remember this - the choice is always in your hands. Your career is a journey that you are meant to drive, not just be a passenger in. Don't be afraid to take detours, explore uncharted territories, and make bold choices. After all, these experiences create an enriching, fulfilling, and successful career.

This decision propelled me on a rollercoaster ride that shifted my career from the side seat to the driver's seat. Along the way, I tinkered with many exciting projects and even whipped up my PHP-based framework, 'Akaar,' similar to baking a unique flavour of cake in a world full of vanilla. I even made it to the 'Who's Who' of the PHP world by being featured in a popular PHP magazine, https://www.phparch.com. My story exemplifies what can happen when you step up to the comedy mic of your professional journey.

Let's not make this a stand-up comedy show where I'm the only one talking. Let me share some secret ingredients that spiced up my career dish. Buckle up as we're about to embark on a joyride!

The Comedy Sketch of Your Career

Evaluate your current sitcom: Like a comedy sketch, your career needs some self-reflection. Identify your punchlines (strengths) and flop jokes (weaknesses). I noticed my punchline was my strong base in web development, and my flop joke was that I wasn't into server-side technologies as much as I'd have liked. So, I decided to make PHP the main character of my career sitcom. By doing so, you too can make your career sitcom a blockbuster hit!

Choose your comedy genre:

Whether it's slapstick, dark, or romantic comedy, every comic has a preferred genre. The same goes for your career. For example, I didn't just focus on PHP but went all-in on PHP-based frameworks, which helped me cook up 'Akaar.' Your preferred genre will help you leave a memorable impression on your audience.

Master the art of improvisation:

In comedy, a good improv can save a dying sketch. Similarly, in your career, mastering the required skills can save you from professional stagnation. To truly 'get' PHP, I tried my hands on projects as diverse as the types of coffee in a hipster café. I also played around with different PHP-based open-source projects like a child in a sandbox.

Don't just be a comic, be the comic:

Let people know that you're not just a one-show wonder. Show them that you're here to stay. Share your knowledge and expertise with the community just as I did when I wrote articles about my experiences with PHP and 'Akaar.'

You could also try starting a blog, recording video tutorials, hosting webinars, or giving presentations at industry events.

Leave your comedic signature.

Like how comedians have their signature jokes, you need something that sets you apart from the crowd. My work on 'Akaar' was my signature act, demonstrating my ability to innovate and develop a unique solution. But don't worry; you don't have to do a crazy stunt like pieing yourself in the face. Simple things like obtaining certifications, participating in hackathons, or contributing to open-source projects can be your signature.

Networking

Remember when you tried to tell a joke, and nobody laughed because they didn't get it? That's what it feels like when you're in the wrong network. Try attending conferences and meetups to exchange ideas with people who speak your language. Virtual coffee chats in online forums and social media platforms can also help you establish your reputation.

The joke that never gets old

In the programming world, trends change faster than the punchline of a comic joke. To stay relevant, keep yourself updated with the latest developments in your area of expertise. In my case, I followed industry trends, read articles, and learned about emerging technologies related to PHP.

Before I forget, remember to work on your brand. Think of it as your comic persona that resonates with your audience. Strengthening your brand is similar to crafting your comedic style. A website or a blog can serve as your virtual comedy club where you showcase your expertise. Being active on social media platforms, contributing on GitHub, participating in discussion forums, and sharing valuable content consistently can also help you define your comedic style.

You could even try taking centre stage at industry events, publishing research or case studies, obtaining advanced certifications, collaborating with other thought leaders, or seeking media exposure. It's all about how you tell your joke - your unique journey and expertise.

As the famous programmer Donald Knuth once said, "People who are more than casually interested in computers should have at least some idea of the underlying hardware. Otherwise, the programs they write will be pretty weird." So, step into the limelight, share your jokes (knowledge), and laugh your way up the professional ladder. After all, your career is your stage, and it's time to deliver your punchline!

Amazing! You're now in the driver's seat, controlling your professional journey. But beware of the upcoming speed bump - 'Intellectual Arrogance.' It's an enticing road that often leads astray. Are you ready to navigate this tricky path and stay grounded? Steer carefully; your journey into the next chapter awaits!

CHAPTER XXIII

Intellectual Arrogance – The Most Dangerous Skill!

""Knowledge is power" - Sir Francis Bacon"

"Knowledge is power," wrote Sir Francis Bacon, but let's not forget that great power comes great responsibility. As you navigate the complexities of your career, amassing knowledge and expertise, it's vital to remain grounded and open to continuous learning.

Unfortunately, as we ascend the ladder of professional success, we often risk developing intellectual arrogance, a pitfall that can undermine our growth and relationships.

The picture is as vivid as a scene from a blockbuster movie: the hero, once the cherished beacon of hope and intelligence, starts behaving as if they are the only repository of wisdom. They start to dismiss valuable advice from their trusted allies, ignore the wisdom of mentors, and reject constructive feedback. This is not an uncommon scenario in real-life professional contexts.

Intellectual arrogance can be particularly harmful in the IT industry, where technologies evolve rapidly and learning never stops. The belief that one has reached the pinnacle of knowledge and expertise often leads to complacency and stagnation. It is, in many ways, a career-limiting move.

In this chapter titled "Intellectual Arrogance - A Dangerous Downfall in Your Career," we will delve into the concept of intellectual arrogance, its impact on your career, and strategies to avoid this pitfall. Drawing from my experiences and observations, I hope to shed light on the importance of maintaining humility and a learner's mindset throughout your career.

Remember, the journey of knowledge is infinite, and every person we meet has something new to teach us. In the wise words of Socrates, "The only true wisdom is in knowing you know nothing." Let this philosophy guide you as we explore the intriguing landscape of intellectual arrogance.

As we bask in the glow of our newfound authority and expertise, we often forget to watch our step. Let me share a tale from my early days as a Team Lead. High on the thrill of my promotion, I acted like a general, ordering my team around, dismissing my colleagues' inputs, and arguing with clients as if my opinion was the only one that mattered. I half expected to be handed a crown and cape for my royal parade around the office!

It wasn't long before I woke up from this power-induced stupor and realized that the world of tech isn't a monarchy, and I wasn't its reigning queen. Countless tech wizards were out there, and my journey had just begun.

Regrettably, intellectual arrogance is an affliction that many talented engineers fall prey to, damaging their careers and relationships. As they say, "If you're the most intelligent person in the room, you're in the wrong room." This chapter aims to help you recognize and navigate this pitfall to ensure your success story doesn't turn into a cautionary tale.

Intellectual arrogance isn't just about having a big ego. It's a complex beast that takes different forms. It could manifest as a dismissive attitude towards others' opinions, an aversion to learning from others, defensiveness when challenged, or an inability to accept feedback gracefully. Even seemingly harmless actions, like talking more than you listen, can be signs of this toxic trait.

Intellectual arrogance is like an unchecked superpower. It isolates you, stunts your growth, and can tarnish your reputation. Worse still, it can creep into your leadership style, creating a negative, autocratic environment that disengages your team.

Fret not; for every villain, there's a hero; in this case, that hero is you. We'll discuss strategies to recognize and combat intellectual arrogance. These include cultivating empathy, embracing diverse perspectives, celebrating others' success, engaging in continuous learning, and embracing the beauty of making mistakes. Remember, even superheroes have weaknesses.

Reflecting on your actions, building a supportive network, and setting realistic expectations can help keep your ego in check. After all, even the most outstanding experts have limitations and are always learning.

As Socrates once wisely put, "I know that I am intelligent because I know that I know nothing." Let that be your mantra as you navigate your journey through the ever-evolving landscape of technology. So, buckle up and get ready to dive into the complex world of intellectual arrogance, your most dangerous foe in the realm of expertise.

Let's look at the signs of intellectual arrogance in the mirror of introspection. When you dismiss others' ideas without considering them, that's your first red flag. You might also discover you've developed a stubborn refusal to learn from others, a trait that's about as helpful as a chocolate teapot.

Do you become defensive when your ideas are challenged?

Or even worse, do you start resembling a grumpy cat whenever you're given negative feedback?

Don't even start on the classic sign of intellectual arrogance: speaking more than listening. If you're doing all the talking, who's doing all the learning?

Of course, no one wants to be around a know-it-all, so this behaviour tends to push people away, leaving you in a lonely fortress of solitude. Your growth gets as stagnant as a pond with no outlet, and your reputation takes a nosedive faster than a skydiver without a parachute.

However, fret not, my fellow tech enthusiasts. We're not doomed to become like comic book villains, forever imprisoned in our intellectual arrogance. We can arm ourselves with powerful strategies to combat this potentially destructive trait.

First off, remember to practice empathy and compassion, not just with your code but with the people around you. Engage with people with different viewpoints and experiences, even if they disagree with you on whether Python is better than Node.js.

Secondly, celebrate the success of others. There's no harm in a little cheerleading, and it could help ground your ego. It's like they say, "The only time you should look down on someone is when you're helping them up."

Thirdly, never be afraid to ask for help. It shows humility, opens up learning opportunities, and, let's face it, it's always fun to see the perplexed expression on a colleague's face when you ask them a tricky question.

In addition, commit to lifelong learning. Don't just rest on your laurels. Attending workshops, conferences, and online courses can not only expand your knowledge but also expose you to diverse perspectives.

Regular self-reflection is also crucial in this battle against intellectual arrogance. Take the time to evaluate your actions, attitudes, and interactions. As they say, "A man who refuses to admit his mistakes can never be successful."

Building a supportive network and setting realistic expectations also play a crucial role in avoiding intellectual arrogance. Remember, no one is perfect, and everyone has something to learn. As Albert Einstein said, "Once you stop learning, you start dying."

So, my fellow tech enthusiasts, let's keep these strategies in our arsenal as we venture further into the exciting world of technology. By avoiding intellectual arrogance, we can build a more collaborative, respectful, and innovative tech community. Because at the end of the day, no matter how smart you are, teamwork makes the dream work!

Intellectual arrogance is a dangerous pitfall, isn't it? But you've passed it with flying colors. Now, it's time for a big leap. Do you feel the adrenaline rush? Brace yourself; we're about to take flight!

CHAPTER XXIV

Ready to fly:- Prepare yourself for a big jump in your career

"Stay committed to your decisions, but stay flexible in your approach." - Tony Robbins.

We are about to embark on a journey redefining your professional trajectory. It's the exciting chapter of preparing for a quantum leap in your career. Brace yourselves!

Throughout this journey, we've conquered the intricacies of the IT industry, escaped the treacherous quicksand of intellectual arrogance, and geared ourselves with an arsenal of technical skills. Now, it's time to spread our wings and prepare to soar. It would be best if you had more than technical expertise to leap forward in your career.

What we're about to discuss are skills that are often overlooked in formal education. They're the 'soft skills' - the human element of the corporate world. Though they might not appear as a requirement in job descriptions, they are what sets apart a good programmer from a great leader in the technology industry.

As we stand on the precipice of this big jump, I encourage you to keep an open mind, ready to unlearn, learn, and relearn. Because when it comes to career growth, it's not just about how high you can fly but also how well you can adapt and soar in the ever-changing winds of the professional landscape.

Let's start with Coding Mastery. "Mastery? But I've already aced that," you might think. But no, my friend, coding mastery isn't a one-time affair. It's like hitting the gym for your coding muscles. You've got to be persistent and consistent. Keep flexing those muscles by reading standards, learning from others' code, contributing to open-source projects, and utilizing AI tools like ChatGPT and CoPilot. Think of it as keeping up with the Joneses in coding.

Next, we come to Multitasking and Creativity. As you advance in your career, juggling tasks becomes as essential as juggling semicolons in your code.

And creativity? It's not just for artists and musicians. When implementing business logic or improving your code, thinking outside the box can lead to innovative solutions that set you apart from the crowd.

Stepping up, we encounter Leadership. Here's a secret - Leadership isn't about ruling over your minions from a throne but nurturing more leaders. It's about transferring knowledge and supporting your team. The most outstanding leaders don't create followers; they create more leaders. Remember, your knowledge isn't meant to be hoarded - it's meant to be shared.

Then there's Peer Communication. It's no secret that, as tech folks, we aren't always the most gregarious. But communicating effectively with peers is paramount in a team environment. Remember, asking for help isn't a sign of weakness; it's a sign of being human.

With communication comes the inevitable - Conflict with Peers. Like a nasty bug, conflicts do creep in. But knowing how to handle them can be the secret debug tool in your kit, reducing their intensity and sometimes even resolving them.

Finally, we reach Taking Ownership and Responsibility. This isn't about adopting a puppy; it's about standing up and saying, "I've got this." Yes, ownership can be scary and often take you out of your comfort zone, but that's where the magic happens. Without taking ownership, you might find your career idling on the runway instead of soaring through the skies.

Take my experience as an example - when I joined a leading company, they didn't have the expertise or infrastructure to start open-source software development. So I stepped up to set up the infrastructure and the team for a new department, even though I had no prior experience. I took ownership and responsibility, and 15 years later, they had a thriving department.

Taking these skills onboard doesn't just prepare you for the next giant leap in your career; it prepares you to fly. It's about moving ahead in your career and soaring to heights you've always dreamt of. So, buckle up, keep your seat upright, and prepare for takeoff!

But wait, here's an extra nugget before you ignite those engines - Continual Learning. Even as you take the pilot's seat, remember the world around you is dynamic and evolving at an alarming speed. Staying on top of new technologies, frameworks, methodologies, tools, languages, and industry trends. Engage in continuous learning through workshops, webinars, conferences, and online courses. This is the fuel that keeps your engines roaring and your career soaring.

Remember, your cabin crew - your peers, subordinates, and superiors - are as crucial to your journey as you are. Embrace a collaborative approach, ensuring the success of both your flight and that of your fellow passengers. Communicate, share, and resolve conflicts with empathy and understanding.

At the risk of overusing the flight metaphor (too late?), don't forget to use your safety equipment - your Support Network. Surround yourself with individuals who can offer constructive criticism, help you navigate turbulence, and hold you accountable for your actions. They are your co-pilots, ready to help you stay on course.

To conclude, the cockpit of success in your career doesn't require you to be a superhero. It requires humility, a hunger for knowledge, a commitment to collaboration, and the courage to take risks. By fostering these skills, you're not only preparing for a quantum leap in your career but also for a successful and satisfying journey.

As you're about to hit the runway, remember the words of the legendary computer scientist Grace Hopper, "The most dangerous phrase in the language is, 'We've always done it this way.'" To fly, my friend, you've got to be ready to do things differently, to learn, and most importantly, to leap.

Great job! You've taken a big leap. Now, it's time to navigate job transitions. It's like a chess game, with every move making a big difference. Ready to play the game?

CHAPTER XXV

Career Milestones: Navigating Job Transitions

""The old rules are crumbling and nobody knows what the new rules are. So make up your own rules." - Neil Gaiman."

Life is about constant evolution, and your professional journey is no exception. Each step along the path contributes to your career's continuous growth and development. But now and then, you arrive at a crossroads where you must make a significant decision. Knowing when and how to transition to a new job is one such critical juncture.

Think of your career as a series of investments of your time, skills, and aspirations. And just like any wise investor, the trick lies in discerning when to hold on and when to diversify your portfolio.

Leaving your first job, that 'comfort nest', to step into the unknown can seem daunting. However, it's important to remember that growth often requires embracing change. This chapter aims to guide you in navigating this crucial crossroad, helping you determine when you're ready for a job change and how best to approach it.

The signs that it's time for change can be subtle. Your first job will always be particular in your heart, just like your first love. But, as in any relationship, when the growth stagnates, the passion wanes, and you feel like you're going through the motions, it might be time to take a step back and reevaluate.

As you delve into this chapter, let's remember the words of Neil Gaiman. In this ever-changing world, it's up to you to make your own rules. So, gear up, fasten your seatbelts, and prepare for this exhilarating journey towards new professional horizons!

Evaluating your growth

Just like in a committed relationship, evaluating your personal growth within your first job is essential. Are you still learning, being challenged, and expanding your skillset? It might be time to consider moving on if you find yourself stuck in a professional rut or feeling unfulfilled.

Picture this: You've been at your first job for a while, and it feels like Groundhog Day - the same tasks and projects. It's as if you're living the movie on repeat. While Bill Murray had a good time, you want something more exhilarating and fulfilling in your career.

Defining your goals

Similar to knowing what you want in a life partner, defining your career goals is crucial. What direction do you want to take? What skills do you want to develop? Setting clear goals allows you to narrow your job search and find opportunities that align with your aspirations.

As in a romantic relationship, having shared goals and visions for the future is crucial. In your career, this means knowing where you want to be and what steps to take to get there. It's like planning the perfect proposal - you need to know where you want to go before you take that leap.

Researching the job market

When you're ready to take the plunge into a new job, it's essential to research the job market. Stay informed about industry trends, in-demand skills, and emerging technologies. This knowledge will empower you to make informed decisions about the type of job that suits your interests and ambitions.

Think of it as attending a speed dating event. You want to know who's in demand, what qualities they're looking for, and how you can stand out from the crowd. Researching the job market is like getting a sneak peek at the dating pool before deciding which potential suitors to pursue.

Assessing company culture

As you want a partner who shares your values and complements your personality, finding a company with the right culture is crucial. Consider work-life balance, professional development opportunities, and a supportive environment that aligns with your career goals.

Imagine going on a series of blind dates where the potential partners have vastly different values and lifestyles. Finding a company whose culture and values resonate with your own is essential. After all, you'll be spending a significant amount of time together.

Networking and connections

In both love and career, connections play a vital role. Expand your professional network, attend industry events, and engage in online communities. Networking can open doors to hidden job opportunities, introduce you to like-minded professionals, and provide valuable insights into potential employers.

Networking is like having a wingman or wing woman by your side. They can introduce you to potential matches (job opportunities), vouch for your qualities and skills, and offer guidance as you navigate the dating scene... I mean, the job market!

Evaluating job offers

As the saying goes, "With great job offers come great decisions." When you receive job offers, looking beyond the superficial aspects like salary and benefits is essential. Consider the growth potential, learning opportunities, and overall fit with your long-term career goals. Remember, you're not just committing to a job but to a future.

Think of it as receiving multiple marriage proposals. You wouldn't accept one solely based on the size of the diamond ring, right? You'd consider factors like compatibility, shared values, and a promising future together. The same applies to job offers - it's about finding the right fit for your professional journey.

Recognizing the signs

Sometimes, it's clear when it's time to move on. Perhaps the company culture no longer aligns with your values, or you've hit a glass ceiling in growth. Pay attention to the signs that indicate it may be time for a change.

Consider this scenario: You're in a relationship where your partner constantly undermines your ideas and stifles your growth. It's time to realize your worth and seek a partner who appreciates and supports your ambitions. Similarly, if your current job prevents you from reaching your full potential, it may be a sign to explore new horizons.

Planning your exit

Leaving your first job requires careful planning and a respectful approach, like ending a relationship. Give proper notice, complete any pending tasks, and maintain professional relationships. Remember, the world is small, and you never know when your paths may cross again.

Leaving a job is akin to having a mature breakup conversation. It's about expressing gratitude for the experiences, sharing your intentions, and parting ways amicably. Burning bridges will only lead to regret and hinder prospects.

Embracing new challenges

Once you've decided to move on, embrace the opportunities that come with a new job. Step out of your comfort zone, be open to learning, and take on challenges to further enhance your skills and knowledge.

Think of it as going on a blind date with a stranger who is your perfect match. You're excited, nervous, and ready to explore a new dynamic. Embracing new challenges in your career is like discovering the hidden gems and possibilities that await you.

Leaving your first job and pursuing new opportunities is a significant decision that can shape your career. It's like finding the perfect partner who supports and motivates you to achieve your dreams. Remember, just as in love; it's essential to evaluate your growth, define your goals, research the job market, assess company culture, network, and make informed decisions. Making the correct choice sets the stage for a fulfilling and successful career.

Here's a questionnaire to help you reflect on your first job and make informed decisions about your career:

1. What are your long-term career goals, and how does your current job align with them?

1. Have you experienced personal and professional growth in your current role? If yes, how? If no, what factors have hindered your growth?

3. Do you feel fulfilled and challenged in your current position or long for more?

4. Have you reached a point where your learning curve has plateaued, and there are limited opportunities for advancement?

5. Does your current job provide a positive and supportive work culture that aligns with your values?

6. Have you explored all avenues within your current company to further your career, such as training programs, mentorship opportunities, or internal transfers?

7. Are you receiving fair compensation and benefits relative to your skills, experience, and industry standards?

8. Are you passionate about the work you're doing, or do you feel a lack of enthusiasm and motivation?

9. Have you considered the potential growth and learning opportunities offered by other companies in your industry?

10. Are you ready and willing to step out of your comfort zone and embrace new challenges to accelerate your career growth?

Take your time to reflect on these questions and evaluate your current situation. Remember, there's no one-size-fits-all answer, and the decision to leave your first job should be based on your unique circumstances and aspirations.

As the great philosopher Socrates once said, "The secret of change is to focus all of your energy, not on fighting the old, but on building the new." So, embrace the change, seize the opportunities, and embark on a new chapter of your professional life. Your career awaits its happily ever after!

As we wrap up our journey through the detailed roadmap of navigating job transitions, it's crucial to remember that these career milestones mark significant growth phases.

You've learned to recognize, adapt, and embrace these transitions. But what lies beyond these transitions? How does one shift from being a part of the team to leading one?

This is precisely what we explore in our next chapter, 'Servant Leader - The Most Important Role in Your Entire Career.'

We will delve into the heart of leadership and the transformation it entails. How does one embody the values of a servant leader? Are you prepared to undertake this profound journey into leadership?

CHAPTER XXVI

Servant Leader – The Most Important Role in Your Entire Career

""The best way to find yourself is to lose yourself in the service of others." - Mahatma Gandhi*"*

From exploring the importance of empathy, we are now about to venture into another pivotal chapter of our professional journey - embracing the role of a Servant Leader. Although it might sound strange or paradoxical at first, this transition is a natural progression that combines your technical expertise and empathy to place you at the helm of leadership.

In IT, leadership extends beyond the conventional definitions of power and control. It isn't about assuming authority or commanding obedience. Instead, it revolves around facilitating growth, understanding team dynamics, and, most importantly, providing service and support. This unique approach to leadership gives rise to the concept of 'Servant Leadership', a seemingly contradictory term yet profoundly meaningful.

As we journey through this chapter, we'll dissect the concept of Servant Leadership, understand its significance in the IT world, and explore how to imbibe its principles in your role as a leader. I assure you, it's not as daunting as it sounds. So, strap in, open your mind, and get ready to step into the shoes of a Servant Leader, potentially the most influential role in your entire career.

Let's begin by understanding what servant leadership truly entails. The term 'Servant Leader' was first coined by Robert K. Greenleaf in his seminal 1970 essay "The Servant as Leader". He explains that a servant leader is a servant first, making a conscious decision to lead to better serve others, not to garner power for personal gain. This leadership style turns the traditional power leadership model upside down, focusing on empowering the team, addressing their needs and facilitating their performance.

The world of IT is replete with examples of servant leadership, but one individual stands out for his remarkable application of this philosophy - Satya Nadella, CEO of Microsoft. Since assuming the role of CEO in 2014,

Nadella has successfully reimagined Microsoft's corporate culture, transitioning from a mindset of "know-it-all" to "learn-it-all". His focus on empathy, learning, and employee development is a testament to the power of servant leadership.

To be a successful servant leader in IT, here are vital skills and attributes to nurture:

1. **Empathy**: At its core, servant leadership is about putting the needs of your team first. Understanding their perspective, their challenges, and their aspirations are key. It involves acknowledging your team members' diverse backgrounds and experiences and treating everyone with equal respect. Empathy builds trust, fosters open communication, and strengthens your team.

2. **Communication Skills**: As a leader, you're often the link between stakeholders - from team members to management to clients. Clear, concise, and thoughtful communication is crucial. It's not merely about passing on information but also about active listening. A servant leader listens to understand, not just to respond. It's through such deep understanding that innovative solutions and ideas often emerge.

3. **Leadership Skills: In servant leadership, leadership isn't about exerting control but** setting the direction and creating an environment where people can thrive. This involves setting a vision, inspiring your team, making decisions, and displaying integrity. It means walking the talk and leading by example.

4. **Project Management**: A project's success depends on management in IT. Being able to plan, execute, and oversee projects effectively is crucial. This involves setting realistic goals, allocating resources wisely, managing timelines, and mitigating risks. As a servant leader, you are also responsible for shielding your team from external pressures and letting them focus on their tasks.

5. **Ownership:** Servant leaders are responsible for their team's successes and failures. They take accountability for the decisions and actions taken and are willing to admit mistakes. They understand that failure is a part of the journey and use it as an opportunity to learn and grow.

6. **Client Management:** IT is often a client-centric field. Understanding the client's needs, setting and managing expectations, and ensuring client satisfaction is vital. Servant leaders excel in this aspect because their service-oriented mindset extends to

7. How to Get Updates and Reports from the Team: A servant leader knows that gathering updates and reports is not about micromanagement. It's about keeping everyone aligned towards a common goal. The leader establishes a non-intrusive yet effective process, respecting team members' autonomy while keeping track of progress.

Every servant leader is different yet shares the same fundamental values and priorities.

They empower their team, fostering an environment of trust, cooperation, and mutual respect.

They place service before self, recognizing that their success lies in their teams' success.

They lead not from the front but from within the team, always ready to offer advice or encouragement.

"servant leadership is all about making the goals clear, rolling your sleeves up, and doing whatever it takes to help people win. In that situation, they don't work for you; you work for them."- Ken Blanchard.

So, as you step into the world of leadership, take a moment to reflect - are you ready to be a Servant Leader?

The evolution from an individual contributor to a Servant Leader in IT is both an honour and a challenge. It requires constant growth and adaptation. But as you journey through this path, remember the essence of servant leadership. In serving others, you'll find not just the respect and admiration of your team but also the fulfilment and purpose that makes a truly great leader.

Remember the words of Lao Tzu, an ancient Chinese philosopher often considered the father of servant leadership philosophy - "The highest type of ruler is one of whose existence the people are barely aware... When his task is accomplished, and things have been completed, all the people say, 'We have achieved it!'" This is the epitome of servant leadership – a leader who makes their presence felt through the success and fulfilment of their team. And this is the kind of leader you can aspire to be. The journey is challenging, but the rewards are immense.

Embrace this role, foster these skills, and watch as you leave a significant imprint on your team, your organization, and the field of IT.

FantaYou'veYou've grasped the essence of the most importantyou'llyou'll ever play in your career - being a servant leader. But what do you think makes a servant leader genuinely effective? Could it be empathy, perhaps? Aha!

We will explore that in the next chapter, "The Pillars of Servant Leadership in IT: Starting with E"pathy". Ready to dive deep into the ocean of empathy, the first essential pillar of servant leadership?

CHAPTER XXVII

The Pillars of Servant Leadership in IT: Starting with Empathy

"Empathy is seeing with the eyes of another, listening with the ears of another and feeling with the heart of another." – Alfred Adler.

In our journey so far, we've ventured into various terrains of the IT industry, unearthed valuable insights and uncovered pivotal roles. One such significant role is that of a Servant Leader. Servant Leadership, although universal, holds particular resonance in the IT world.

Among the many facets of Servant Leadership, there lies a gem at the heart - Empathy. We've waded through the waters of empathy before, acknowledging its value and impact. However, when we place empathy under the spotlight of Servant Leadership, its essence takes on a greater significance.

In this chapter, we delve deeper into the role of empathy in Servant Leadership, exploring its impact and how it serves as a cornerstone for the other aspects of this leadership style.

As a servant leader, empathy goes beyond understanding team members' emotions or problems. It is about actively engaging with them, offering genuine support, and working together to overcome challenges. If a member of your team is feeling down or lacks confidence in their task, this is where you, as a leader, step in.

You sit down with them, maybe even put a hand on their shoulder if appropriate, and say, "Let's solve this together." This simple gesture can be incredibly empowering for a team member who is struggling. It shows them that they are not alone, that their leader is there to support them, and that their contribution is valued.

Remember, the IT industry is brimming with individuals who possess a strong desire to excel. They are driven by the thrill of solving complex problems, the joy of learning new technologies, and the satisfaction of seeing their code come to life. Yet, like anyone else, they can experience moments of doubt, confusion, and burnout. These are the moments when your empathetic leadership can make a significant difference.

By being there for your team members, by offering genuine support and guidance, you can help uplift their spirits and reignite their passion. This, in turn, creates a positive work environment, one where everyone feels valued and motivated.

As an IT Servant Leader, your role is not just about driving projects to completion or ensuring the code is free of bugs. It's about empowering your team, helping them overcome challenges, and facilitating their growth. It's about leading with empathy, understanding, and respect.

The role of a Servant Leader in IT can be challenging, but with empathy as one of your guiding principles, you can navigate these challenges with grace and effectiveness. The first step towards becoming a Servant Leader in IT is developing empathy - for your team, for their challenges, and for the human element in the world of technology.

In the following chapters, we will further explore the other pillars of Servant Leadership in IT, but remember, no matter what skill you're focusing on, empathy should always be at the core of your leadership style. It is the foundation of Servant Leadership, the trait that distinguishes a good leader from a truly great one.

In the words of John C. Maxwell, "People don't care how much you know until they know how much you care." As a Servant Leader in IT, let your empathy be your beacon, guiding you as you steer your team towards success.

You've built strong pillars for your leadership, beginning with empathy. Yet, there's another unexpected key to effective leadership - communication. Curious to know how these seemingly disparate skills intertwine? Continue your journey and find out!

CHAPTER XXVIII

Journey Through IT: Communication – An Unexpected Key in Servant Leadership

""The art of communication is the language of leadership." - James Humes.*"*

Embarking on my journey in the IT realm as an eager, freshly-minted programmer, my head was full of ambitious dreams, and my heart was ready to take on any challenge that came my way.

My mind was a sponge, ready to soak up all the knowledge of the expansive programming ocean.

Yet, my initial voyage into the professional sea ushered me into uncharted waters - the realm of customer communication. This random assignment blew like an unanticipated gust in my planned trajectory. Confronted with conversing in a language, not my native tongue, the task was daunting.

However, rather than retreating into the cocoon of familiar tasks, I chose to adopt the spirit of an adventurer, embracing this unforeseen responsibility as a golden opportunity for learning. As the unexpected protagonist in the saga of Servant Leadership, I realized that communication is not just about exchanging information - it's about understanding the emotions and intentions behind that information.

In this chapter, I'll recount my voyage through the compelling currents of effective communication in the context of Servant Leadership and how this seemingly daunting task transformed into an unexpected key, unlocking countless opportunities in my professional journey.

My initial interaction with the customer was nerve-racking. However, I realized that while my English might not have been perfect, my technical skills and the ability to convey my understanding of their needs mattered most. I understood their requirements, analyzed their problems, and proposed efficient solutions. This direct interaction not only helped me better understand their needs but also enabled me to build a rapport with the customer.

My lack of fluency in English did not deter me. Instead, I used my strengths – my technical knowledge and problem-solving skills – to communicate effectively. I understood the importance of clear and concise communication in conveying complex technical concepts to clients. I practised, I prepared, and I performed.

I worked diligently, ensuring every aspect of the project was executed flawlessly. And at every step, I kept the customer in the loop, explaining the process, the challenges, and the solutions in a language they understood. My consistent communication with the client, coupled with the successful execution of the project, won their trust and appreciation.

After a decade of working in the company, I decided to move on to explore other opportunities. Upon my departure, the same client, whose first project I had worked on, shared with the company's management that despite receiving more cost-effective proposals from others, my communication skills convinced them to entrust the task to our team.

They recognized that I understood their requirements technically and built a relationship based on trust and respect. A combination of my technical acumen, sales skills, and the ability to articulate the customer's needs effectively sealed the deal.

This early experience taught me a valuable lesson - that communication is not just about language proficiency. It's about understanding the other person's perspective, establishing a connection, and building trust. It's about listening, understanding, and responding effectively. It's about conveying your knowledge and ideas clearly and convincingly.

My story is not unique. Many of you might have faced similar situations in your careers. However, the important takeaway is never to underestimate the power of good communication. No matter how complex your technical skills are, they are of little value if you cannot effectively convey your ideas and solutions. Remember, your technical expertise might get you the job, but your communication skills will help you succeed.

In the following chapters, we will delve deeper into the importance of effective communication in the IT industry. We will explore strategies and techniques to improve your communication skills and provide real-world examples to illustrate these concepts.

You've discovered the hidden key - communication. But, like a prism, communication has multiple facets. Ready to polish this prism and master the spectrum of communication skills? Your journey awaits in the next chapter.

CHAPTER XXIX

Polishing the Prism: A Personal Journey to Master the Spectrum of Communication Skills

""The single biggest problem in communication is the illusion that it has taken place." - George Bernard Shaw"

Within the vibrant canvas of Information Technology, the necessity of a broad skill set is as critical as a compass for a mariner charting unexplored waters. Your arsenal of abilities, spanning technical prowess to managerial competencies, forms the rich tapestry of your professional identity. However, amidst this array of expertise, one skill acts as the linchpin - communication.

Communication isn't just the oil that lubricates the well-oiled IT machinery; it's the cog that bridges the chasm between innovative thoughts and their implementation. The harmonious symphony orchestrates your interaction with clients, teammates, and stakeholders.

Over the years, one truth has become clear to me: the soul of communication lies not merely in 'what' you express but predominantly in 'how' you relay it.

In this chapter, I'm excited to invite you to my journey of honing communication skills. We'll navigate the multifaceted labyrinth of this crucial competency, sharing tools and strategies from my personal experience to help you polish this prism to its utmost brilliance in your professional arena.

However, as we set sail, I feel it's essential to articulate a friendly disclaimer: The anecdotes, suggestions, and strategies I present here are based on my experiences and understanding.

While I've tried to be comprehensive, my perspective is inherently limited, and I do not claim to provide specific or professional advice. So, take what resonates, and feel free to adapt it to your unique situation. After all, we're all explorers charting our unique course in the vast ocean of communication skills.

In the previous chapter, we delved into empathy, a cornerstone of servant leadership. But effective communication stretches beyond empathy, encompassing an array of facets that I'll share, rooted in my journey.

Listen Actively: Back when I cut my teeth in the industry, a pattern emerged. Being an e-commerce veteran, I was privy to the industry's ins and outs. It came to a point where I felt I could anticipate the client's needs before they could articulate them. This assumption was based on my accumulated knowledge and the consistency of the client's needs. However, I soon realized that this mindset was a potential pitfall.

Each client interaction presents a unique narrative, and it's our responsibility to pay close attention to their distinctive requirements. They are the heroes of their stories, and their enthusiasm and passion should reverberate through our conversations. As a listener, we must make them feel heard and understood. It's akin to a physician's role, where despite solid inkling of the patient's ailment based on the symptoms, they meticulously listen to the patient before arriving at a diagnosis.

Be Clear and Concise: As tech enthusiasts, we find solace in our jargon-filled universe. Our language brims with intricate terms and complex phrases that explain the tech marvels we create. We often forget that for many of our clients, these terms could be perplexing or intimidating.

In my early career years, the excitement of sharing every technical detail about a project often got the better of me. Only with experience did I realize that my clients were looking for solutions rather than a crash course in tech jargon. It's essential to keep the technical lexicon to a minimum and focus on providing our clients with clear, concise, and relevant information.

Adapt to Your Audience: Communication is as much about adaptation as it is about transmission. The key is to meet the clients where they are. This philosophy was instrumental in winning my first project.

Despite not being completely fluent in English, I could convince the American client to trust our services. It wasn't my command over the language but the combination of my technical prowess, sales acumen, and willingness to understand and cater to the client's needs that helped seal the deal. A simple gesture like maintaining eye contact can exhibit your confidence and sincere interest in the client's project.

Show Empathy: Displaying empathy towards your clients helps establish a meaningful relationship. There will be instances when a client's budget might not align with your services. In such cases, show understanding and offer alternative solutions to help them.

Once, a prospective client had a limited budget significantly less than our standard rates. Rather than turning them away, I suggested they work with a freelancer who could provide services within their budget. This act of empathy not only offered them a solution but also left a positive impression on our organization, leading to future collaborations when they had larger budgets.

Ask for Feedback: Encouraging client feedback throughout the project fosters an environment of open communication and demonstrates your commitment to their satisfaction. Simple prompts such as "Do you agree?" or "Do you have any suggestions for improvement?" can facilitate open dialogue and ensure alignment between their expectations and your deliverables.

Practice Regularly: Like any other skill, communication gets refined with continuous practice. When I was a newbie in this vast IT landscape, resources were not as easily accessible as they are today. Tools like AI or Netflix were unavailable to facilitate English language learning. However, we made the best use of the available resources and continuously strived to improve.

If speaking English is a hurdle, don't shy away from practising. I often randomly called customer support lines to talk to English, unaware that my fluency wasn't perfect. But guess what? That's okay. Every stumbling conversation is a step towards fluency. The key here is to practice, practice, and practice some more.

In conclusion, communication is a broad umbrella covering various aspects - active listening, clarity, conciseness, audience adaptation, empathy, soliciting feedback, and regular practice. Remember that effective communication is about transmitting your ideas and understanding others, showing empathy, and fostering an environment conducive to open discussion.

Looking back, I can confidently say that my communication skills have driven my success. The first project I won was a testament to effective communication's power, which held proper throughout my journey. The next chapter will delve into specific tips and tricks to hone verbal and written communication skills within a team and with clients. The goal is to help you craft your own success story, one conversation at a time.

You've polished the prism of communication and mastered its spectrum. But did you know communication also includes the spoken word? Next up, we dive into the realm of verbal communication. Ready to speak up?

CHAPTER XXX

Mastering Verbal Communication – My Insights

"All the world's a stage, and all the men and women merely players"
- William Shakespeare.

If life is a play, consider this chapter the part where I don the mask of a language maestro - an expert in the art of verbal communication! (Ha! If only...)

But seriously, folks, here's the lowdown. As a non-native English speaker navigating the IT industry, I've been thrust onto this global stage, my lines written in the universal language of business - English. And let me tell you; it's been quite the comedy of errors!

I have taken a few liberties just as Shakespeare took poetic license in his work. In this chapter, I share my journey – a roller coaster ride of blunders, faux pas, and the occasional triumph - in the realm of verbal communication.

But remember, I'm not claiming to be a linguistic virtuoso or an expert in communication. The anecdotes and insights I present here are personal, gleaned from the school of hard knocks, not an ivory tower of theoretical knowledge.

So as you read on, take my tales as they are - humble experiences from a fellow traveller on this winding road called 'career in IT'. Let's get this show on the road, shall we?

Communication is an art, a crucial component of success in any industry, and IT is no exception. Here, I share my personal observations and strategies I've developed over years of interacting with international clients. While English is not my first language, I've honed my communication skills to bridge cultural and linguistic gaps. I present my golden rules for effective verbal communication, understanding these are not exhaustive and, more importantly, these are born from my personal experiences.

Speak Slowly and Clearly: Remember the time when you learned to ride a bicycle? You started slowly, right? Similar is the approach when English isn't your first language. Speak slowly, and articulate your words carefully, ensuring each syllable is heard. Do not rush through sentences. Elevate your voice just enough to be audible, but avoid shouting. Remember, the goal is to be understood, not to finish first.

Take a Pause: Imagine reading a book without punctuation marks. Confusing, right? Similarly, pauses are the punctuation marks of verbal communication. They give you and your listener time to process the information. Use pauses to your advantage - they portray you as a thoughtful and considerate communicator.

Wait for Completion: Ever been interrupted while speaking? Frustrating. Avoid doing the same to others. Allow the speaker to complete their thoughts. It's a sign of respect and shows you value their input. Not only does this prevent misunderstanding, but you also might learn something new in the process.

Ask Questions: Picture yourself in front of a painting; unless you're the artist, you can't know the exact intent behind it. Likewise, in communication, instead of assuming, ask questions. For example, when discussing a project, seek confirmation about critical decisions - "Are you suggesting we use Node.js for this project? Are you confident that it's the best fit?" This leaves no room for misunderstanding.

Maintain Eye Contact: Ever had a conversation with someone who is constantly looking at their watch or phone? Annoying, right? Eye contact, whether on a video call or in person, demonstrates engagement and respect for the other person. It sends a clear message: "I'm here, I'm listening, I'm with you".

Correct Pronunciation: Ever had your name mispronounced? It feels awkward. Always strive to pronounce names correctly. When I had a client named Louis, I went on YouTube and learned the correct pronunciation before our call. This effort shows respect and professionalism.

Time Zone Awareness: Picture a good morning greeting at night in your location - sounds odd, right? Be mindful of your client's time zone and greet them accordingly. This small detail conveys respect and consideration for your client's local schedule.

These tips are merely drops in the vast ocean of communication skills. While they are not comprehensive, they've proven effective in my personal experience. However, improving your communication skills is a continuous journey.

There are countless resources, including YouTube videos and online courses, that can aid you in this journey. I encourage you to dive into them. After all, it's not about having perfect English; it's about being an effective communicator.

Congratulations on honing your verbal communication skills! Now, let's shift gears and explore written communication. Are you ready to wield the mightier sword - the pen? Or should I say, the keyboard?

CHAPTER XXXI

Mastering Written Communication – My Personal Insights

*"**"**Writing is its own reward." - Henry Miller.**"***

Oh, I wish this quote resonated with me when I was knee-deep in writing bug reports and email updates at 2 AM! Alas, as glorified as it may seem, written communication can sometimes be as appealing as doing laundry (No offence to laundry enthusiasts!)

Welcome to the chapter where I take you on a wild ride through my adventures (or misadventures) in the magical realm of written communication. From the peaks of crisp, well-crafted emails to the depths of ambiguous project updates, we're going on a roller coaster of tales, lessons, and confessions.

But before we embark dear reader, here's a small disclaimer: I am no William Shakespeare or J.K. Rowling. My experiences are as accurate as they come, rough around the edges, and, most importantly, they're mine. I've not studied at the prestigious universities of the written word, but I've learned from the tough streets of the IT industry, where every word written carries weight.

So, buckle up, and brace yourselves for a journey into the unfiltered world of written communication in IT, as seen through my humble lens. Spoiler alert: It's not all quills and sonnets!

Written communication carries significant weight in the information technology world, where interactions frequently occur virtually. It can make or break an exchange, influencing a customer's perception of you and your entire team or organization. The effectiveness of your written words can be more impactful than your verbal skills, especially if you are in a non-managerial role, where much of your communication may be through written mediums like emails, Slack, Trello, or ClickUp.

Let me share the strategies for effective written communication I've developed over the years.

1. **Use Language Tools:** In my early career days, I relied heavily on Microsoft Word and Outlook to check spelling before sending emails. Today, even after two decades of experience, I religiously use Grammarly to ensure my emails are grammatically correct before sending them. While non-native English speakers may receive some leeway, consistently poor English can become a hindrance over time. Today, we have the power of advanced AI tools like ChatGPT, which can help you draft professional-level English. Remember to review and proofread the AI-generated text for unintended errors or inaccuracies.

2. **Ask Questions:** Just as I mentioned in the previous chapter about verbal communication, asking questions is equally, if not more, critical in written communication. Despite your confidence in understanding the situation or task, it's wise to seek confirmation. Even if you express your perspective or judgement, framing it as "Based on my experience..." or "This is what I think..." leaves room for constructive dialogue.

3. **Write Concisely:** The beauty of effective written communication lies in its brevity. Be it in an email or a report, keep your sentences short and your paragraphs concise. Tools like Grammarly and AI can help maintain brevity and clarity. A well-structured email, with quick, straightforward sentences, will always be more impactful than a long, convoluted paragraph.

4. **Reference and Conclude:** The starting and ending of your communication carry significant weight. Always start your conversation with respect if applicable, making it easier for the recipient to track the context. Similarly, concluding your message effectively is vital. A properly completed statement could summarise your points, provide a Call-to-Action (CTA) such as "I will call you tomorrow" or "Awaiting your reply," or offer an invitation for further questions.

5. **Proofread:** The 'Send' or 'Submit' button can be quite tempting, but resist the urge until you've thoroughly proofread your text. It's essential to ensure your message is clear, concise, and error-free before it reaches its intended recipient.

Just as in the previous chapter, these tips are not exhaustive. Plenty of resources are out there to help you improve your written communication skills further.

Remember, communication is the bridge between you and your clients, colleagues, and stakeholders. Ensuring this bridge is strong will undoubtedly pave the way for your success. The upcoming chapter will explore some technical skills essential for IT professionals.

You've mastered the art of written communication, turning complexity into simplicity. But what about asking the right questions? In the tech world, inquiry is an art too. Let's unlock its power in the next chapter.

CHAPTER XXXII

The Art of Inquiry: Unlocking the Power of Questions in Tech

"Judge a man by his questions rather than by his answers." - Voltaire.

Yes, we've been down this road before. We've talked about asking questions in previous chapters. We've touched on its importance and explored how it can improve communication and understanding. But here we are again, dedicating an entire chapter to it.

Why, you may ask? Because, dear reader, the humble act of asking questions deserves more than just a mention. It is a skill that has served me well throughout my professional journey, helping me navigate challenging conversations and build stronger relationships. Hence, it's only fair to delve deeper into it.

Ah, the art of asking questions. My secret weapon, my Excalibur in the often tumultuous realm of technology. You might be thinking, "Isn't this just basic communication skills?" Ah, but that's where the magic truly lies!

Imagine you're stuck in one of those meetings, where the air is heavy with potential conflict and clashing egos. You're confident you have the correct answer, or perhaps you're convinced your viewpoint is the definitive one. Yet, you don't just blurt it out; instead, you craft a thoughtful question, allowing others to pause, reflect, and reevaluate their perspectives.

My dear reader, questions are the humble yet mighty champions of peace. They disarm confrontation, quell the raging ego, and open up a dialogue, turning a potential battlefield into a roundtable of knowledge exchange.

We are humble explorers charting unfamiliar territories in the vast cosmos of IT, where none can claim to know it all. There's always something new to discover, someone new to learn from - a colleague, a client, or a stakeholder.

Here are a few magical phrases that have served me well: "Are you sure?" "Could you please advise?" "Are you suggesting this?" "Can we also consider this?" "Should I recheck this?" Now, I'm not promising miracles with these phrases. They might need a little tweaking depending on the situation, the person, or even the day of the week!

And, before we delve deeper, allow me to don my disclaimer hat (I bet you're used to it by now!). As always, I'm no sage or an oracle, just a humble developer who has gathered these nuggets of wisdom from the school of hard knocks, where every project, and every interaction is a new lesson. And let's be honest, the last thing I want is to sound intellectually arrogant, claiming to have all the answers. I mean, wouldn't that defeat the whole point of this chapter? So, let's dive into the beautiful, understated art of asking questions with humility and respect at the core!

Indeed, there's an art to asking questions, especially in the IT professional world. It's a technique that fosters open communication, encourages dialogue, and can help de-escalate potentially tense situations. However, like any skill, it takes time, practice, and a pinch of finesse to master. In this chapter, I hope to share some of my insights and personal experiences on how asking questions can transform your interactions, fuel growth, and build meaningful relationships.

Let's begin by understanding why asking questions is so integral.

Why Ask Questions?

Firstly, it's crucial to understand that asking questions is not a sign of ignorance or incompetence. On the contrary, it demonstrates a willingness to learn, an openness to others' perspectives, and a maturity to acknowledge that you may not have all the answers.

In the realm of IT, where knowledge is vast and constantly evolving, being open to learning is the key to staying relevant. By asking questions, you allow yourself to learn from other's experiences and insights, thus expanding your own knowledge and understanding.

Moreover, asking questions can help you build rapport and trust with colleagues and clients. It shows that you value their opinions and insights, thus fostering mutual respect and understanding.

The Art of Asking Questions

Now that we've established the significance of asking questions, let's delve into the art of asking the 'right' questions. The 'right' question doesn't necessarily mean the most intelligent or insightful one. Rather, the question facilitates understanding, encourages dialogue, and furthers the conversation.

When asking a question, consider the following:

1. **Be Clear and Concise:** Make sure your question is easy to understand and straight to the point. Avoid unnecessary jargon or overly complex language.

1. **Be Genuine:** Ask questions that you genuinely want answers to. Your sincerity will shine through, showing you genuinely care about the answer.

3. **Be Respectful:** Remember that everyone's perspective is valuable. Ask questions in a manner that shows you respect the other person's opinion, even if you disagree.

The Magic Phrases

Here are a few of my favourite 'magic phrases' that have proven effective in fostering open and respectful communication:

- "Could you please explain that in more detail?"
- "What are your thoughts on this?"
- "Could we consider this from a different angle?"
- "How did you arrive at this conclusion?"
- "Could you help me understand your perspective better?"

Remember, these phrases are merely tools to aid you in your interactions. The real magic lies in your intent, openness, and respect for others' perspectives.

In the words of the great Albert Einstein, "The important thing is not to stop questioning." So, keep asking, keep learning, and keep growing!

And as always, let me cap this off with a humble disclaimer: These are insights gathered from my journey. Different approaches work for different people in different situations, so take these with a grain of salt, and most importantly, continue to find your way!

You've unlocked the art of inquiry, haven't you? Brilliant! What if I told you there's a quest you might be interested in? A quest to be liked, perhaps even loved. Intrigued? Turn the page!

CHAPTER XXXIII

The Quest to be Liked: Becoming the Most Loved Employee in Your Organization

""A good character, when established, is not easily overthrown and is a heritage given to a child which money cannot buy." - Rachel L. Carson.*"*

Over the last few chapters, we've extensively explored essential technical skills, communication strategies, and the 'developer mindset.' You must be thinking, what next? Well, my friend, we've journeyed a long way. Still, we need to complete a critical piece of the puzzle - becoming an invaluable asset to your organization, the one who's not just respected but also loved!

This chapter might not exactly feature in the 'Conventional IT Manual,' but trust me when I say this, it can make a world of difference. It's not about becoming the 'Most Loved Employee' overnight or becoming an 'Office Sweetheart.' No, it's about something far more substantial.

Drawing from my experiences, oscillating between an 'Average Joe' and a 'Charismatic Charlie,' let's delve into this intriguing journey towards being the 'Go-to Employee.' Remember, as always, these are my personal insights and observations, not a definitive guide. Let's see where this path takes us!

Substantial evidence of my position in this spectrum was the steady upward curve of my salary graph. Every year, as if by magic, it almost doubled. Not because I hit the lottery but because I had discovered a simple yet potent secret recipe. And today, I'm ready to share that with you: the magic potion of Commitment, Honesty, Integrity, Courage, Ownership, and a big, infectious Smile.

Commitment: There's an incident that I vividly remember from my days at one organization. A colleague once pointed out how I often had loud discussions in meetings. To him, I explained, it was not arguing but a passionate discussion fueled by commitment. I was fully invested in my work, which often made me fiercely protective of my ideas. This commitment exuded confidence and resulted in me being taken seriously, earning respect and love.

Honesty & Integrity: This one's a no-brainer, but you'd be surprised how many overlook it. Honesty in your work and having integrity can win hearts faster than you can imagine. At one of my previous jobs, I had the opportunity to handle a sensitive project. It was a testing period, and my honest efforts and principled approach reassured my bosses. Not only did they trust me with more responsibilities after that, but our relationship also strengthened.

Courage: Stepping outside your comfort zone can be scary but showing courage can set you apart. In one of the leading companies I worked for, I was offered to set up an entirely new department for open-source software development. It was an area I had little experience in, but I took the plunge. It wasn't easy, but this courage to accept and take responsibility significantly impacted my career and made me a favourite.

Ownership: When you take ownership, you're accountable, putting you in the spotlight. You become the go-to person, the problem solver, the reliable one, and before you know it, you're respected and loved. My taking charge of the open-source project was a prime example of this.

Keep Smiling: Now, this might seem trivial compared to the other points, but believe me, it's the cherry on top. A genuine smile can make you approachable and likeable. My mantra has always been to greet everyone with a big, friendly smile. It breaks the ice, sets a positive tone for interaction, and, most importantly, it's infectious.

As you put these pieces together, you'll find that these simple yet powerful traits can create a ripple effect of positivity and respect around you, making you the most loved employee. Remember, being loved is not about pandering or popularity; it's about mutual respect, trust, and a positive aura people enjoy being around. And when all is said and done, you get the last hearty laugh!

Congratulations! You're on your way to becoming the most loved employee. But how about making the final leap in your IT career? The plunge awaits. Let's dive in!

CHAPTER XXXIV

Taking the Plunge: Timing and Executing the Final Leap in Your IT Career

""Change is the end result of all true learning." - Leo Buscaglia."

In our journey, we've discussed various facets of your IT career - technical skills, communication, teamwork, mindset, and even about becoming a loved employee. Now, we stand on the precipice of a significant turning point - the final leap in your IT career.

Indeed, dear reader, we are now entering the final frontier of our discourse - the decisive and often daunting choice of knowing when and how to make that final leap. It's like standing at the edge of a cliff, overlooking an expansive ocean, preparing to dive into its depths.

This chapter might feel like an adrenaline rush - exciting, anxiety-inducing, and laced with a hint of trepidation. But fret not, for we'll navigate this together. Through my personal experiences and many missteps, I aim to provide valuable insights that could guide you in making this pivotal decision. Remember, these insights are based on my journey and do not constitute professional advice.

Let's brace ourselves for this exhilarating ride!

The Big Fish, Bigger Pond Scenario

My professional journey has had its fair share of twists, turns, and full-circle moments. One such moment was my leap from a smaller, cosier work environment to the colossal realm of IBM. Let me paint you a picture of my thought process.

It all started with a clue, a bubbling thought that perhaps it was time for me to step onto a larger stage. Imagine the thrill of watching an indie band in a cosy bar and then suddenly getting the chance to see a stadium concert with thousands of roaring fans. The prospect was as enticing as it was intimidating.

So, I made the switch without much contemplation and advice-seeking from peers. I jumped headlong into IBM, relishing the opportunity to be a part of a company that has been a benchmark in the industry. It was akin to joining the grand league, a once-in-a-lifetime opportunity.

Working at IBM exposed me to a fascinating work culture, a structured approach to complex problems, and an opportunity to travel abroad, specifically to the US. But, as irony would have it, I wasn't particularly keen on that perk.

Soon, I realized that while IBM was a fantastic place to focus and deepen my knowledge in specific domains, it was not quite the right fit for me. My ambitions were aligned towards understanding the entire business process spectrum - sales, accounts, IT support, networking - the whole nine yards. I yearned to comprehend every cog in the machine, which was not a possibility in a large corporate setting.

So, the moral of this part of my story is if you are contemplating leaping a larger organization, take the time to consider what it means for you and your career goals. If broad, in-depth exposure to multiple aspects of the business is your aim, you might find the experience a bit limiting.

However, suppose you desire to specialize in a specific area, delve deep, and have the opportunity to work with a diverse, global team. In that case, a leap to a larger organization may be a golden opportunity for you.

Dive into Freelancing

Now, let's swing the pendulum to the other extreme. Picture this: you've just woken up, still in your cosy pyjamas, sipping on a steaming cup of coffee, and you're at work. No traffic, crowded buses or trains, or shared office microwave with its cacophony of assorted food smells. Sounds tempting, right? This is the freelancer's life - at least one side of it.

I had a few friends who decided to leave the traditional job market and dive headfirst into the freelancing world. Let me assure you, these folks were as ambitious as a squirrel in an unattended bird feeder. Yet, after a few years, they decided to swim back to the safer shores of a full-time job.

Let's rewind and dive into the 'why' here. As an IT professional, freelancing can seem like a panacea. It offers freedom, flexibility, and a break from the monotony of a 9-to-5 job. But here's the catch: freelancing is like being your own tiny start-up. You are the CEO, but also the accountant, the HR manager, the janitor, and the intern who has to do all the work.

You need to scout for new clients, negotiate contracts, handle all tech issues that arise (because who else will do it?), and manage your taxes. It's a veritable one-person circus; you must be a proficient juggler. On top of all this, you'll probably miss the camaraderie of an office environment, coffee-break chats, and teamwork's joys (and woes).

Sure, there are platforms like Upwork or Freelancer.com to help you find projects, but remember, competition is as stiff as a starched shirt on these platforms. You must outshine a global pool of talented individuals, which can sometimes feel like trying to perform a Shakespearean monologue at a rock concert.

So, if you're contemplating the freelance route, weigh the pros and cons carefully. Ask yourself, "Am I ready to run the whole show? Can I handle the solo performance?" Remember, it's a different tune you'll be playing, and it may or may not be music to your ears.

In the next part, we will look into becoming an entrepreneur - my personal favourite path, akin to signing up for a roller coaster ride in the dark. Buckle up!

Becoming an Entrepreneur

Alright, let's dig into this one, my personal favourite. But beware, this is not for the faint of heart. Becoming an entrepreneur is like deciding to start a rock band. It's thrilling, cool, something you constantly tell yourself you will do "one day". But it's not all jamming and concerts once you're in the band. There's a lot of hard work, sweat, and sometimes even tears.

My journey towards entrepreneurship was a bit like a romantic comedy. There were ups and downs, missteps, and plenty of "Will they? Won't they?" moments. But here's the spoiler alert - I did become an entrepreneur and wouldn't change anything about my journey.

Entrepreneurship can feel like being the captain of your own pirate ship. You're in charge, you make the decisions, and you get to say things like, "All hands on deck!" (Okay, maybe not that last part.) But remember, being a captain means you're responsible for the ship and your crew. Every decision you make will directly impact your business. It's thrilling but also daunting.

Like that time when I had to choose between two projects. One was as tempting as a delicious pizza but had a higher risk, and the other was more like a safe but boring salad. I went for the pizza (of course) and had a bit of a tummy ache afterwards. You see, making decisions is hard. But as an entrepreneur, making hard decisions is a part of your job description.

Another point to remember is that entrepreneurship is a commitment. It's like getting a puppy. It's fun and exciting at first, but you'll have to clean up some messes, put in the time to train them and be ready for some sleepless nights. If you're a 9-to-5 person who loves their weekends free and needs a steady paycheck, this path might not be for you.

But if you're ready for an adventure, prepared for a challenge, and willing to trade in some stability for the ride of your life, then hoist the sails, my friend, and welcome aboard!

Congratulations! You've taken the plunge, but this is just the beginning. A whole new adventure awaits one that might lead you to your dream job abroad. Excited to embark on this journey? Flip the page!

CHAPTER XXXV

Adventure Awaits: Getting Your Dream Job Abroad

""Jobs fill your pocket, but adventures fill your soul." - Jamie Lyn Beatty"

Pack your bags, folks! We are about to take off on a new adventure, this time, overseas. If you've ever caught yourself daydreaming of exploring new places, cultures, and work environments, or if you're like me, who treasures a collection of different currencies just because it's cool (I knew I couldn't be the only one!), then this chapter is just for you.

Ah, the United States of America, the land of opportunities, skyscrapers, and let's not forget, oversized burgers! Who among us hasn't fantasized about working amidst the bustling streets of New York or the high-tech offices of Silicon Valley at least once? Or perhaps you're enchanted by Europe with its rich history, captivating architecture, and a myriad of languages that sound like music to your ears. Or, your sights may be set on the exotic Down Under, working alongside our Aussie friends amidst their vibrant culture and picturesque landscapes.

I assure you that whatever destination has been fuelling your dreams, procuring a job there is not just a move for your career; it's the beginning of an unforgettable adventure. As thrilling as it might sound, navigating the course to your dream job abroad requires careful planning, preparation, and a handful of practical tips. This chapter is dedicated to unfolding the secrets to this exciting journey. Fasten your seat belts; we're ready for takeoff!

There's just something about working in a foreign country that's undeniably exciting. The thrill of experiencing a new culture, meeting people from different walks of life, and not to mention the sheer joy of converting your salary into your home country's currency and feeling like a millionaire (until you convert it back, of course!).

But before you pack your bags, remember that working in a different country isn't just about the glitz and glamour. It's also about adapting to new work culture, understanding different professional etiquettes, and occasionally getting lost in translation. It's like being a fish out of the water and then realizing you must learn how to climb trees!

Let me share a funny incident with a friend who moved to the US for work. At a grocery store, he asked an attendant where he could find capsicums. The attendant looked puzzled and said, "Cap-what now?" After a few minutes of confusion and a quick Google search, they laughed. Turns out capsicum is called 'bell pepper' in the US!

But hey, don't let these little challenges deter you. After all, every new experience is a chance to learn and grow; besides, these funny incidents make for great party stories!

Remember, though, as much as we might fantasize about living in a different country; it's also essential to keep your personal and social responsibilities in mind. Evaluate if this is what you truly want and if it aligns with your life goals. The critical question is whether you can make it work and if it will make you happy.

Well, that's all for this part of the journey, folks! Up next, we have something equally exciting and daunting. Don't worry, it's not a riddle, but it does involve some heavy decision-making. So, take a breather, hydrate, and gear up because we're about to explore the next big decision in your IT career!

We've now journeyed through the delightful pathways of career transitions, dodged a few cobwebs, navigated some winding roads, and hope to emerge with a clearer understanding of the IT landscape. We've laughed, we've questioned, and hopefully, you've found some insight that resonates with your own career aspirations.

In the spirit of ending on a high note, I'll leave you with this quote from the renowned businessman and investor, Warren Buffet, who said, "In the world of business, the people who are most successful are those who are doing what they love." So, whether it's a leap to a larger organization, embarking on a freelancing adventure, stepping up to entrepreneurship, or packing your bags for a job abroad, remember this - do what you love, and success will follow.

But hey, don't take it just from me, or Warren Buffet, for that matter. Explore, experiment, and find your own path in the versatile IT arena. Because, in the end, as the famous author of 'The Alchemist', Paulo Coelho, put it, "It's the possibility of having a dream come true that makes life interesting."

Basking in the thrill of your overseas adventure? Now let's turn the tables and consider a new perspective - the entrepreneurial path in IT. Intrigued? Let's dive in!

CHAPTER XXXVI

Turning the Tables: The Entrepreneurship Path in IT

""Entrepreneurship is neither a science nor an art. It is a practice." - Peter Drucker.*"*

Dear reader, if you've sailed with me through this book thus far, you've reached the uncharted waters of entrepreneurship. Brace yourself, for the sea is tempestuous, the path unknown, but the rewards - oh, the tips could be beyond your wildest dreams!

In our last chapter, we danced around the idea of entrepreneurship in the IT world. But given the booming startup culture and the infectious enthusiasm amongst young engineers, I believe it's time to lift the veil on this intriguing journey.

Remember, entrepreneurship isn't a walk in the park; it's run through a jungle - full of unforeseen challenges, heart-racing thrills, and an array of fascinating discoveries. In this chapter, I will share my insights, triumphs, and failures as an entrepreneur in the tech industry. Let me preface this by saying while my experience could provide a glimpse into the entrepreneurial world; it doesn't serve as an all-encompassing guide. Entrepreneurship, after all, is a unique journey for each individual. So, are you ready to venture into this exciting realm?

Think of entrepreneurship as deciding to start a rock band. It's exhilarating, and calm; it's something you brag about at parties with a nonchalant shrug, "Yeah, I'm starting a band". But once you're in it, it's less jamming and gigs, more tuning instruments and dealing with the drummer who forgot his drumsticks at home. It's a lot of work, a smattering of chaos, and yes, sometimes even a downpour of tears.

Now, don't worry. We will dissect this topic in depth in an upcoming chapter, so consider this a sneak peek, a trailer, if you will, for that blockbuster!

My journey towards entrepreneurship was a bit like a sitcom series, filled with hilarious missteps, unpredictable twists, and an array of interesting characters. The highlight? I did become an entrepreneur; I wouldn't trade that season finale for anything!

Being an entrepreneur is a lot like captaining your pirate ship. There's excitement, decision-making, and the occasional urge to shout, "Arr, walk the plank, ye scurvy dog!" Just kidding, we're not pirates. However, it's crucial to remember that you're responsible for your ship and crew as captain. Each decision is yours, and each consequence too.

I recall a time when I had to choose between two projects. One was as tempting as a double cheese pizza but risky. The other was a plain bagel - safe, reliable, but oh-so-boring. So what did I do? I went for the pizza. And let's say I had to face the 'music of the extra cheese.'

However, entrepreneurship isn't just about making decisions. It's a commitment, like getting a puppy. It's cute and fun at first, but there are messes to clean, obedience training, and the occasional midnight barking spree. If you enjoy a steady paycheck and have your weekends to yourself, this may not be the ride for you.

But if you're up for a challenge, ready to face the winds of change, and are willing to swap some stability for a whirlwind adventure, then, my friend, grab your pirate hat and eye patch, and let's embark on this journey together!

But wait, there's more. The IT field isn't just about startups and code. What if I told you there was a whole world out there? That's right. Next, we're looking at working in a new country. So fasten your seatbelts because we're about to take off!

Having learned about entrepreneurship in IT, are you ready to take the helm of your ship? The next chapter is all about running your IT consultancy firm. Prepare to set sail!

CHAPTER XXXVII

Steering the Ship: A Guide to Running Your Own IT Consultancy Firm

"Risk more than others think is safe. Dream more than others think is practical." - Howard Schultz

Welcome aboard, fellow voyagers! After exploring the various terrains of employment, let's take the helm and chart our own course towards entrepreneurship - running an IT consultancy firm. A journey I know intimately well, for it's the one I've chosen, and let me tell you, it has been nothing short of extraordinary.

As the captain of my ship, I can attest to the thrills, challenges, and immense satisfaction this course entails. The freedom I gained was not just to spend more time with family, take vacations, or have fun but to work the way I always wanted. The liberty to ideate, create, and provide solutions to customers in ways that resonated with my vision.

My first product, AppliView - an applicant tracking system, was a testament to this freedom. It was a product born out of an unmet need in the industry, and the appreciation and acceptance it received from customers worldwide were incredibly gratifying.

The freedom also extended to experiments - some successful, some less so. But each venture, each product, offered immense learning. Despite the failures, the freedom to innovate remained a constant, undeterred source of inspiration.

There's a particular joy in creating customized solutions for clients - proving our technical expertise, creativity, and service commitment. It's a satisfaction that is tough to articulate, one that comes from seeing your vision translate into tangible results.

The journey, as you can imagine, isn't always smooth sailing. The seas of entrepreneurship are often turbulent, throwing challenges like cash flow management, employee retention, client conflicts, etc. The balancing act of ensuring timely salaries while maintaining a healthy business operation can be a daunting task.

Yet, despite these rough waters, the journey is enriching. There's a sense of fulfilment in steering your own ship, in carving your path. It's a journey of resilience, creativity, and constant learning. And for me, it's been a journey well worth it.

I can hear your gears grinding from here. "Run my own IT consultancy firm? Isn't that like trying to tightrope walk across a canyon while balancing a stack of plates on my head?" Well, let me assure you, while it certainly has its moments of thrill and challenges, it's not an impossible feat. With the proper knowledge, preparation, and mindset, it can be a rewarding voyage.

In this chapter, we'll dive deep into what it takes to steer your own ship in the vast ocean of IT consultancy. We'll chart the course, anticipate the storms, and perhaps even find some hidden treasure. So, strap in and get ready for a ride into the entrepreneurial wave. Let's chart the uncharted!

Let's take a trip down memory lane. Remember when we were kids, playing with toy cars and dolls, pretending to run our own businesses? We'd make our siblings or friends our employees and dictate orders to them. Ah, the good old days, right? Running your own IT consultancy firm is kind of like that... just with a tad more paperwork and a lot fewer toys.

You're probably wondering, "Why on earth would I want to do that?" Well, my friends, running your firm means calling the shots, making the big decisions, and occasionally wearing a superhero cape (metaphorically, of course... unless you want to wear one. No judgment here). It's a journey of self-discovery, resilience, and more caffeine consumption than you ever thought possible.

Now, hold your horses. I'm not saying everyone should run off and start their own IT consultancy firm. Oh, no, not at all. This is a journey for those with the courage to face the unknown, those who aren't afraid to leap into the abyss, those who eat challenges for breakfast, and those who don't mind the occasional sleepless night. The entrepreneurial journey isn't for the faint-hearted. It's like a roller coaster ride - sometimes thrilling, sometimes terrifying, but always unforgettable.

You may be shouting, "Okay, okay, I get it! But what's the secret sauce to running a successful IT consultancy?" Well, to be honest, there's no one-size-fits-all answer. But don't worry; I'm not going to leave you hanging. We'll dedicate an entire chapter to this topic later in this book. So buckle up because it's going to be one wild ride!

Right, I think that's enough adrenaline for one day. Remember, always be true to yourself if you decide to jump into the international job market, become a freelancer, or start your own IT consultancy. Your career journey is your own; every path you take is another chapter in your story.

You've steered the ship masterfully, but the journey isn't over. Sometimes, the path can take an unexpected turn. Why should you think twice before launching your start-up? Turn the page to find out!

CHAPTER XXXVIII

An Unexpected Turn: Why You Should Think Twice Before Launching Your Start-up

" "Before you start up, start over" - Ben Horowitz "

Beware, dear readers; we are about to venture into the somewhat turbulent waters of the startup world. This chapter is designed to give you a slightly different perspective that you might not typically come across in the overly optimistic world of entrepreneurial advice. If you will, a stark warning that the startup path is not always a bed of roses.

Why am I spouting such heresy, you ask? Because I've walked that path. I've traversed the unpredictable terrains of entrepreneurship, experienced the thrill of victory, and endured the agony of defeat. I've worked with the big fishes in the corporate pond, including names as significant as IBM, before I decided to swim against the current and don the entrepreneurial hat with my IT consultancy.

Indeed, the startup journey offers its own set of exciting opportunities and challenging lessons. It's a thrilling ride filled with abrupt turns and unexpected stops. This chapter'll explore why you should pause, reflect, and perhaps think twice before embarking on your startup journey. It's time to buckle up; this ride could get a bit bumpy.

Allow me to share my hard-learned lessons, which might make you reconsider before embarking on this daring adventure:

The Cool Quotient:

If you're looking to start a business solely to enhance your "cool" factor, I've got some news: the startup world is less about being glamorous and more about long hours, overflowing inboxes, and endless cups of coffee. Remember, a successful entrepreneur is not born out of the desire to impress others but of passion and a commitment to solving a problem.

The Freedom Fallacy

I once dreamed that my startup would give me plenty of free time. The reality? It felt like I had a newborn baby that demanded my attention 24/ 7. If you envision entrepreneurship as a pathway to long holidays and more family time, you might want to give it a second thought.

The Stability Seeker

Craving stability and predictability? Well, entrepreneurship might not be for you. The life of a startup owner is akin to a roller-coaster ride - thrilling but filled with unexpected twists and turns.

The Responsibility-Phobic

If the thought of assuming responsibility for everything scares you, you might find entrepreneurship a bit daunting. As a startup owner, you are the captain, the crew, and sometimes even the ship itself!

Are You Fond of Your Weekends?

If your idea of a perfect weekend is curling up with a good book, binge-watching your favourite series, or going for a long drive with your loved ones, then the startup life might not be for you. Weekends? Holidays? Vacations? The entrepreneurial world often treats these words as if they're in an alien language. Remember, a startup is like a newborn baby. It demands attention 24/7. And guess what? It doesn't take weekends off.

Risk-averse, are We?

Remember the game 'Snakes and Ladders' we used to play as kids? You might climb up the ladder one moment, only to be swallowed by a snake the next. Such is the world of entrepreneurship. It's a gamble where you bet your time, money, and mental peace, hoping for a jackpot that may or may not arrive. If you prefer a steady income and a predictable routine, this high-risk, high-reward game may not suit your style.

Jack of All Trades, Master of None?

Starting your business often means wearing multiple hats - you're the CEO, accountant, marketer, customer service executive, and sometimes, janitor. You might be a programming wizard, but are you prepared to tackle accounting, sales, marketing, and HR? If you're unwilling or ready to step out of your comfort zone and learn new skills, the startup life might be a tough nut to crack.

Are you a People Pleaser?

As the owner of a startup, you'll face criticism and rejection more often than you'd like. From investors dismissing your ideas and customers complaining about your products to employees grumbling about their workload - you'll see it all. You might struggle in the entrepreneur's seat if you find it difficult to handle criticism or say no when needed.

Patience isn't your Virtue?

Biz Stone, the co-founder of Twitter, said, "Timing, perseverance, and ten years of trying will eventually make you look like an overnight success." Yes, you read it right - TEN years. Success in the entrepreneurial world isn't instant. If patience isn't your strongest suit, the journey might be too long and tiresome.

Do you value your peace of mind more than anything else?

If peace of mind is your ultimate goal and you're content with what you're doing, you may want to think twice before plunging into the unpredictable world of startups. Startup stress is natural, my friends. From managing finances to meeting deadlines, dealing with customer complaints, and retaining employees, the list of worries can sometimes seem endless. It's like a circus juggling act. One wrong move and everything comes crashing down. So, if you prefer a stress-free life, entrepreneurship might be a challenging path for you.

Are you a perfectionist?

The world of startups is messy. It's about trying, failing, learning, and repeating the process until you get it right. As an entrepreneur, you often have to make do with "good enough" because there's rarely time or resources to aim for perfection. So, if you're bothered by the smallest errors and imperfections, be prepared for sleepless nights.

Now, am I trying to dissuade you from starting your own business? Absolutely not. Am I asking you to consider the challenges and introspect whether you're ready for them? Absolutely yes.

Entrepreneurship is a beautiful journey filled with learning, growth, and, yes, success. But, it's important to remember that it's a journey that demands considerable commitment, resilience, and sacrifice.

In conclusion, starting your own business is a path laden with obstacles and uncertainties but can also lead to unimaginable growth and rewards. If you think you have the stomach for this roller coaster ride, by all means, hop on. But remember, just like any roller coaster, there will be ups and downs, twists and turns, and yes, the occasional loop de loop.

My friend, the choice is yours. As the legendary Steve Jobs once said, "Your work is going to fill a large part of your life, and the only way to be truly satisfied is to do what you believe is great work. And the only way to do great work is to love what you do." So, if you're ready to embrace the chaos and live the dream, then strap in and get ready for the ride of your life.

But if you've read through these points and think, "Hmm, maybe this isn't for me," that's perfectly fine, too. As I always say, everyone has their own path to success. Maybe your path isn't littered with the rubble of startups but paved with the stability of a regular job. And guess what? That's more than okay. After all, we can't all be Elon Musk, can we?

You've taken an unexpected turn in your stride, but knowing when to start your startup or business is crucial. Are you ready to time your leap? Let's delve deeper!

CHAPTER XXXIX

When to Start Your Own Start-up or Business?

""Twenty years from now, you will be more disappointed by the things that you didn't do than by the ones you did do. So throw off the bowlines. Sail away from the safe harbor. Catch the trade winds in your sails. Explore. Dream. Discover." - Mark Twain*"*

Dear reader, in our last chapter, I might have come across as a bit of a party pooper, seemingly throwing a wet blanket on your entrepreneurial dreams. If you felt that way, please accept my humble apologies. I did not intend to discourage or dissuade you from embarking on this exciting journey. Quite the opposite. My goal was merely to provide a balanced perspective, a clear view of the challenges you might face, based on my experiences.

After seemingly portraying myself as a doomsayer in the previous chapter, I now don my optimist's hat to highlight why you should consider launching your own startup. The thrill, the exhilaration, the sense of accomplishment, and, of course, the inevitable challenges - they're all part of the package. And believe me when I say it's a package worth unwrapping.

The entrepreneurial journey has been my chosen path, and despite its ups and downs, I wouldn't have it any other way. And so, I present this chapter to you, my friend, as a window into why I chose this path and why you might also want to. So, let's hoist the sails and embark on this thrilling voyage together!

My journey started back when I was a budding Chemistry major. I found myself enchanted by Visual Basic as I danced joyfully, seeing my first program - a simple "Hey Chirag" button - come to life on the screen. That was when the coding artist in me was born. Since then, I've tried to solve business problems using technology, even when it wasn't part of my job description. My projects ranged from project management tools to 'no code' platforms. Some might call these ventures fruitless, but I see them as my foundation stones, shaping my approach to problem-solving and fuelling my entrepreneurial mind.

Now, let's consider some essential factors, based on my experience, that indicate you're ready to start your own IT business. If you can identify

113

with the following points, then my friend, you're all set to don the entrepreneurial hat!

Problem-Solving Ability

My entrepreneurial journey has been a playground for my problem-solving abilities. I remember those early days when I'd code in my sleep (almost), developing solutions that would give people a seamless user experience. And you know what? It wasn't because it was my job. I did it because I loved it.

The first program I created was on Visual Basic during my Master's in Chemistry. The program was simple; it would pop up a little greeting saying "Hey Chirag" when you clicked on a button. When I first saw it come to life, I was ecstatic. That tiny button seemed like the key to a magical world of endless possibilities. I felt like I'd just cracked a secret code and couldn't wait to delve deeper into this fascinating world.

And that's when I knew, right there and then, that I was a problem-solver at heart. This realization didn't happen overnight, and I can't say it was like a eureka moment in a bathtub. But it felt as natural and inevitable as a caterpillar turning into a butterfly when it did happen.

Since then, I've embarked on various projects, some out of sheer curiosity and others to provide solutions to real-life problems. I developed a project management product, crafted my own code generator engine, and dipped my toes into the 'no code' platforms in the early 2000s.

Sure, not all these projects saw the light of day, and not all were successful. But you know what? They all helped feed my entrepreneurial spirit and taught me invaluable lessons about problem-solving, persistence, and resilience.

So, if you're like me, someone who sees a problem and gets an irresistible urge to fix it - and particularly if you can envision leveraging technology to do it - you should seriously consider embarking on an entrepreneurial journey.

Seriously, how cool would it be to be a superhero with a keyboard for a weapon, solving problems one line of code at a time? Trust me, the satisfaction you get from creating your solution to a problem is unparalleled. It's like building your miniature Death Star with Raspberry Pi and watching it stand tall and proud, ready to take on the galaxy!

Remember, every startup is essentially a solution to a problem. And if problem-solving is your second nature, then you, my friend, have a head start on this entrepreneurial racetrack. So buckle up and get ready for a thrilling ride!

Communication and Empathy

This one might sound like a soft skill, but it's as critical as your technical abilities, if not more. Communicating effectively and empathizing with others is a cornerstone of entrepreneurship.

You see, in the world of startups, you don't just talk to computers or code all day (though sometimes, that would be nice!). You interact with people. Lots and lots of people. Customers, employees, investors, partners - you name it. And when you deal with people, you need to understand them, their needs, and their concerns. And most importantly, you need to make them feel understood. That's where empathy comes in.

I recall my early days when I was just a programmer. My job was primarily about writing and debugging code. But as I ventured into entrepreneurship, I had to wear multiple hats. I had to pitch to investors, motivate my team, understand customer needs, and manage partnerships. I had to be a salesperson, a leader, a listener, and a comforter all at once.

I remember this one time a customer was struggling with our product. The problem wasn't really with our product, but more about how they were trying to use it. Now, the tech geek in me wanted to say, "Hey, that's not how it's supposed to be used. You're doing it all wrong!" But the entrepreneur in me knew better.

Instead, I put myself in their shoes, understood their frustration, and patiently guided them through the correct process. I didn't just provide a solution; I gave them a better user experience, won their trust, and fostered a relationship. That's the power of communication and empathy.

So, if you're the kind of person who can strike up a conversation with anyone, anywhere, or if you're someone who can understand and feel others' emotions as your own, then entrepreneurship could be your jam! It's like being a talk-show host, a counsellor, and a problem-solver all in one. It's not always easy, but who said being an entrepreneur is a piece of cake? Trust me; it's worth it. After all, solving a customer's problem is excellent, but making a customer feel heard and understood? Now, that's priceless!

People Person

Alright, now this one's a biggie. Ask yourself: Are you a people person? Do you love interacting with people, understanding their perspectives, engaging in healthy debates, or just talking about anything under the sun?

Do you thrive in social settings? If the answer is a resounding yes, then my friend, you have a significant advantage in your entrepreneurial journey.

Entrepreneurship isn't just about having a great idea or building an innovative product. It's also about building relationships. As an entrepreneur, you'll be constantly interacting with a wide variety of people - be it customers, employees, partners, investors, or even competitors. You'll need to communicate your vision, convince people to buy into it, negotiate deals, handle disputes...the list goes on. And being a people person can make all of this a lot easier and, dare I say, enjoyable.

Now, don't get me wrong. I was more of a 'behind-the-scenes' guy. I loved coding and solving complex problems, and I was pretty good at it. But when it came to networking or public speaking, I was about as comfortable as a cat on a hot tin roof.

This one time, early in my entrepreneurial journey, I had to pitch our product to a potential client. Now, remember, I was a programmer-turned-entrepreneur. My idea for a great conversation was to discuss the latest programming languages or debugging techniques. But here I was, trying to sell a product, not to a fellow programmer, but to a non-tech business owner.

I stumbled, I stuttered, I broke into cold sweats. But I pushed through. I focused on the one thing I was good at - explaining the tech behind our product. I discussed how it could solve their problems and improve their business processes. And guess what? They loved it! That was my first successful sales pitch, giving me newfound confidence.

So, even if you're not a people person, don't worry. Entrepreneurship has a way of bringing out skills you never knew you had. You'll learn, you'll adapt, you'll grow. Just remember - people aren't just potential customers or investors. They're, well, people. Treat them respectfully, listen to and understand them, and you'll do just fine.

And if you're already a people person? Well, you're going to have a blast! Trust me, the relationships you'll build, the people you'll meet, the conversations you'll have - they're all part of the exciting, sometimes crazy, but always rewarding journey of entrepreneurship. So, put on your best smile, and get ready to charm the world! Because when you're an entrepreneur, every conversation can be the start of something big.

Embrace Failure

Let's chat about failure. Now, I can almost hear you say, "What? Why would I want to think about failure? Isn't entrepreneurship all about success?" Well, it's about time we had the "failure talk". And trust me, it's not as grim as it sounds.

First, let me clarify - I'm not suggesting that you leap into entrepreneurship with a 'bring on the failure' banner. But, the reality is, in the world of startups, failure isn't just probable; it's a rite of passage. There will be bumps on the road, pitfalls you didn't anticipate, and ideas that don't pan out. And that's okay. What's important is to remember that failure doesn't define you; it refines you.

When I began my entrepreneurial journey, I had this discussion with myself. "What if I fail?" I asked. Well, I had two answers for myself. First, failure wouldn't stop me from programming or pursuing what I loved. It would add more to my experience from a different perspective.

Secondly, I realized that if my venture failed, it wouldn't be 'me' failing. It would be an approach, a methodology, a concept that didn't work out. It would be a lesson learned, a stepping stone to success. That's why I prefer calling them 'fail-lessons', not failures. Sounds better, right?

Once you befriend failure, it becomes less of a dread and more of a guide. Each misstep will offer a unique insight, a valuable lesson. Each stumble will make you more resilient and more determined. And trust me, once you make peace with the possibility of failure, you'll find yourself stepping more confidently into the entrepreneurial ring.

Remember that the road to success is littered with the wreckage of failure. The trick is not to swerve around them but to salvage lessons from them. It's about viewing every 'fail lesson' as a chance to regroup, rethink, and rebound stronger.

So, wear your battle scars with pride, my fellow entrepreneurs. They are proof of the battles you've fought, the challenges you've weathered, and the resilience you've shown. They are a testament to your courage, your tenacity, and your undying spirit. And trust me, and when you finally make it, those scars will be your badges of honour.

Timing is everything when starting your own start-up or business. We've explored the signs to look out for and the considerations to make before taking the plunge. Don't rush the process - let it naturally lead you to the entrepreneurial path. If you're ready to make the leap, do it wholeheartedly. If not, it's okay - great things take time. Now, it's time to move on to something even more important than your career - your life. Join me in the next chapter, "Enjoy Your Life: The Most Important Skill to Grow."

CHAPTER XL

Enjoy Your Life: The Most Important Skill to Grow

""There's no way that you can live an adequate life without many mistakes." - Charlie Munger"

Well, well, well, here we are. We've hopped on the rollercoaster of starting as a programmer, buckled up for the ride to the top, and learned to manoeuvre the tricky loops of the IT world. We've envisioned ourselves sitting in the C-suite as a CTO, creating waves as a founder, or juggling all the balls as an entrepreneur. But as we get ready to get off this rollercoaster, we need to make one final, vital stop: Life Enjoyment Station. Yes, you heard it right!

Remember those childhood days when the biggest worry was deciding whether to get chocolate or vanilla ice cream? Or when the joy of life came from small moments like playing in the park or watching a favourite cartoon? Adulthood may have brought responsibilities and tough decisions, but it shouldn't take away from the pleasure of living.

Despite the allure of success and the ambition to climb the career ladder, let's not forget our old friend, Happiness. After all, what's the point of reaching the top if you can't enjoy the view, right? So, buckle up one more time as we embark on this final ride together to explore the essential skill to grow - the ability to enjoy your life honestly.

Throughout this book, I have shared anecdotes, insights, and advice from my experiences, hoping to offer you valuable guidance on your professional journey. Now, I'd like to share something of a more personal nature. I've always believed that the journey is just as important as the destination, if not more so. Despite the immense focus, we put on our careers, it's important not to lose sight of the things that truly matter: our Happiness and the joy of our loved ones.

You see, I've never embarked on any journey, be it a career move, a startup venture, or a risky business decision that could jeopardize my Happiness or the Happiness of my family. I've spoken at length about the need for resilience, grit, and a willingness to sacrifice for your entrepreneurial dream. However, it's equally important to understand that there's no 'one-size-fits-all' approach.

So, in this penultimate chapter, let's take a deep breath, step back from our intense discussions, and turn our attention to the essential skill we need to master in our lives – enjoying it.

I've seen friends who've put their personal and family lives on the back burner to pursue their business aspirations. And they've reached heights in business that I may never come. But here's the kicker – I don't compare my journey with theirs. They're at the stage they wanted to be, just as I am where I wanted to be based on my priorities.

This brings me to an oft-asked question, can there be balance? The infamous work-life balance – is it achievable in an entrepreneur's life? Is it practical? After all, as an entrepreneur, aren't you implicitly trading off peace and family life?

I don't have all the answers, but I can share the strategies that have worked for me. I may be wrong, but these choices have made me happy and content. And that's all one can ask for, right? Let me share a few fundamental principles I've followed.

Enjoying life isn't just about having fun. It's about finding balance, embracing growth, and nurturing relationships. It's about appreciating the journey, not just the destination. Remember to carry these lessons with you as we wrap up this chapter. Let them guide you in your pursuit of Happiness and success. And now, let's shift gears and focus on another crucial aspect of our lives - our health. Join me as we delve into our next chapter, "Health Matters - Your Prime Asset in the IT Field."

CHAPTER XLI

Health Matters – Your Prime Asset in the IT Field

"Health is not valued till sickness comes." - Thomas Fuller

Dear reader, as we've embarked on this winding journey through my professional life, sharing stories, mistakes, and triumphs, we've come to a very dear chapter. This one comes from a place of personal pain, profound realizations, and immense importance.

I wish I could bold every word, underline each sentence, and highlight every paragraph of this chapter. Because the message here is paramount: Health Matters.

You see, back when I was immersed in my programming career, clocking long and late hours, entranced by the challenge and complexity of codes, I ignored the most valuable asset I had - my health. This negligence led me to pay a hefty price: I was diagnosed with diabetes at an early age. And this wasn't all. The disease brought along a baggage of anxiety, comparison, and a myriad of issues that severely affected my life satisfaction and growth.

I know that in the IT field, our workstyle isn't like most other professions. We don't move around a lot; we sit for hours glued to our screens. This sedentary lifestyle, coupled with poor posture and unhealthy food habits, extracts a significant toll on our health.

I've seen many colleagues suffer from back problems, obesity, and other health issues - occupational hazards of being in the IT field, if you will. I know the pain, and I don't want you to go through it.

Whether you are a budding IT enthusiast or a seasoned professional, consider this humble advice from a fellow traveler: place your health at the very top of your list. It's the most valuable asset you possess.

Now, I'm not suggesting that you should immediately sign up for a gym membership and aim for a six-pack. The goal here is to be 'Active'. The specifics of what that means are up to you. It could be a brisk walk in the morning, a yoga class, or perhaps dancing to your favorite tunes.

I won't get preachy; I simply want to emphasize this point: Prioritize your health. Cherish it. Take care of it. A healthier you is a happier you, a more productive you, a more fulfilled you. And isn't that what we all aspire to be?

Your health is your most valuable asset in the IT field. Don't ignore it or take it for granted. Practice good habits, focus on nutrition, exercise regularly, and don't forget to rest. Remember, a healthy body and a healthy mind are essential for success. As we conclude this chapter, let's take our health and happiness with us as we move forward to the final chapter of our journey, "Final Words."

CHAPTER XLII

Final Words

"There is no end. There is no beginning. There is only the infinite passion of life." - Federico Fellini

As we journey towards the end of this literary adventure, I can't help but reflect on the myriad experiences and thoughts I've shared in these chapters.

First, I'd like to emphasize that this book is not an instruction manual nor a tried-and-tested recipe for success. I am neither an oracle nor a trailblazer who has attained such monumental success that it gives me the authority to dictate absolutes.

Instead, consider this book a narrative, a tapestry woven from the threads of my experiences and perspectives. I embarked on writing this with a humble intent – to share my journey with the young and aspiring programmers and entrepreneurs out there, providing them with a measure of context and perspective.

I hope my tale serves as a mirror that reflects the triumphs and pitfalls I encountered. My ambition is that this reflection helps others steer clear of the mistakes I made or at least face them armed with a little foreknowledge. Some might even draw inspiration from the paths I've trodden and see if those routes align with their aspirations.

In essence, if any part of my journey, any nugget of wisdom, any anecdote, or piece of advice can light the way or offer a modicum of assistance to anyone treading this path, I'd consider the purpose of penning down this book fulfilled. And with this, I bid you adieu, my dear reader, and wish you an exciting journey ahead.

I want to leave young programmers and entrepreneurs with this advice: To be human. Develop empathy. Enjoy life. Dance, sing, play, and spend time with your family.

We're all still trying to understand life's profound truth, but one thing is certain: the success you share with your family and friends will bring you happiness at the end of the day.

Finally, I want to share an insight from Bronnie Ware, an Australian nurse and writer. In her book, "The Top Five Regrets of the Dying," she compiled people's most common regrets in their final days. The regret that topped the list was - "I wish I'd had the courage to live a life true to myself, not the life others expected of me." And one of the other top regrets was - "I wish I had stayed in touch with my friends."

These insights underscore the importance of staying true to oneself and maintaining relationships with friends. The grind of entrepreneurship shouldn't overshadow the significance of living a fulfilling and balanced life.

In closing, dear reader, let's keep this in mind: Success is not just about building profitable businesses but about building lives that we can revisit with contentment.

And with this, we come to the end of our journey together in this book. I hope my experiences, insights, and thoughts have added value to your journey as a programmer or entrepreneur. Keep learning, keep growing, and most importantly, enjoy the ride!

Wishing you the best of luck in all your endeavours.

Chirag Kansara (kansara@gmail.com)

CHAPTER XLIII

Bonus Chapter: The AI Revolution and ChatGPT

"Artificial Intelligence is the new electricity." - Andrew Ng"

As we enter this bonus chapter, I feel a palpable excitement stirring. After all, we're about to delve into a topic that is not only disruptive but also transformative in the tech landscape – Artificial Intelligence. But our focus isn't on just any AI; we'll zoom in on the revolutionary and game-changing version known as ChatGPT.

Picture this – it's the tail end of 2021, and I'm pouring over the initial outlines of this book. I had an inkling, of course, about the significant strides AI was making. Yet, the enormity of the AI wave that would crash onto the shores of 2022, especially for developers and entrepreneurs, was beyond my anticipation.

The relevance and importance of learning and developing skills to navigate this AI-powered terrain cannot be overstated. If you're an entrepreneur or a programmer, understanding and harnessing the incredible power of AI is now an imperative rather than an option.

And it's not just about comprehending the tech behind it. Equally vital is the ability to craft compelling prompts that can unlock the full potential of tools like ChatGPT.

Admittedly, this subject is so vast and nuanced that it could quickly fill a book on its own (and who knows, it might just be my next writing endeavour!). But given the context of our current discourse, it would be a disservice not to address it here, even if only briefly. So, without further ado, let's dive in!

Believe me when I say AI will revolutionise how we code in the next couple of years. It will also render many jobs redundant, and while this may be a bitter pill to swallow, I urge you to face this truth head-on so you're not caught off-guard.

Make it a priority to learn how to leverage AI in your everyday developer or entrepreneurial life. It can assist you in writing code, even conceiving and building entire projects. Amazingly, with the right AI tools, you can even embark on a career as a programmer, even if you have zero prior knowledge of programming.

This is a concept I've explored extensively in a couple of my books. You can check these out on the Amazon Kindle Store by searching my name. These books provide a comprehensive guide to understanding and using AI in your professional life, and I genuinely believe they can help you get a head start in this new era.

As an entrepreneur, this AI magician will prove invaluable in countless areas. It can assist you in designing effective marketing strategies, crafting compelling advertisement copies, creating detailed project management plans, drafting appointment letters and agreements, developing project specifications and requirement documents, and even designing guides for your creative initiatives. The possibilities are truly endless.

The only limitation you'll encounter is the one set by your imagination. So, I urge you to expand your mind, break free from traditional constraints, and prepare to soar to new heights with AI.

The revolution is here, my friends! Brace yourselves and, most importantly, embrace the magic of AI. The future awaits!